No Left Turns

ALSO BY JOSEPH L. SCHOTT

Rails Across Panama
The Ordeal of Samar
Above and Beyond

No Left Turns

Joseph L. Schott

Praeger Publishers · New York

Published in the United States of America in 1975
by Praeger Publishers, Inc.
111 Fourth Avenue, New York, N.Y. 10003

Second printing, 1975

© 1975 by Joseph L. Schott

Library of Congress Cataloging in Publication Data

Schott, Joseph L
    No left turns.

    1. United States. Federal Bureau of Investigation.
.2. Hoover, John Edgar, 1895–1972. I. Title.
HV8138.S32 1975   353.007′4   74-15687
ISBN 0-275-33630-1

Printed in the United States of America

For Tom Carter and Earle Haley and Dwight Bright-
man and all the other denizens of the Field who knew how
to play the game, and for the SAC who understood the
importance of the halo effect.

Contents

No Left Turns

A Parable

The sexual life of the camel
    Is stranger than anyone thinks.
In a moment of amorous weakness
    He tried to make love to the Sphinx.
But the Sphinx's posterior orifice
    Is filled with the sands of the Nile.
This accounts for the hump of the camel
    And the Sphinx's inscrutable smile.

—Author unknown

Special Agent Joseph L. Schott quoted this parable in his farewell address to the employees of the Dallas FBI office on the occasion of his retirement from the Bureau in December 1971.

⬛️⬛️➡️ *1*

Prologue: The Dinosaur in the Backyard

When I retired from the FBI in December 1971 after twenty-three years of service, I did not carry out with me much in the way of memorabilia. On the day I turned in my revolver, badge, credentials, FBI Handbook, and briefcase, the people in the field office where I had worked so long gave me a wristwatch with some engraving on the back. For the information of those generous souls who chipped in fifty cents or a dollar each to help buy this watch I can report that it keeps accurate time and I wear it every day. I have some photographs and some old newspaper clippings in a scruffy-looking file folder, and I have a ten-year FBI service key and a twenty-year key. I have some letters signed "J. Edgar Hoover" in blue ink. No other FBI official at the Seat of Government, better known as SOG in the Bureau, dared use that same colored ink for his own correspondence. I like to think that the Director wrote the signatures himself, but they may have been written by his secretary, Miss Helen Gandy, who had access to his private blue ink. Two of them are letters of "censure" containing denunciations and veiled threats. "You have been exceedingly derelict in your failure to properly handle these matters," says one of the letters in the Director's usual denunciatory style. "Such delinquencies indicate a lack of attention on your part in carrying out your assignments. . . . In the future you will make every effort to avoid such delays and omissions."

Not bad, comparatively. I have seen letters he wrote to others beginning, "I am amazed and astounded and completely at a loss to understand how a supposedly rational human being could commit an act of such colossal stupidity . . ." and then sailing on from there to deeper seas of vitriol.

I have half a dozen letters of the more pleasant kind— letters of "commendation"—alluding to successfully completed cases I participated in, all minor victories in his never ending war against crime.

There is also a letter that accompanied an "incentive award" of $200, "in recognition of your commendable contributions to the Fiscal Year 1970 statistical accomplishments realized by the Dallas Office." I was not sure at the time, and am still not sure, what the commendable accomplishments were, but I didn't send the money back and I don't intend to. I made it a practice during my long Bureau career never to openly question the infallibility of the Director. If he said I deserved the $200, who was I, a cretinous, shaggy-assed Field agent, to argue with him? I accepted the award without the slightest twinge of conscience.

I don't have any of the stuff that some FBI book writers lugged out with them—Xerox copies of official memoranda, pages ripped from the Handbook or the Big Manual, and all sorts of documents that are supposed to prove that Mr. Hoover was a paragon of virtue or a scoundrel, depending on which case they are trying to prove. Most of what I have are personal recollections and opinions. These are not bitter, frustrated, or idolatrous, but they are uniquely mine. No one can take them from me.

In this book the names of all those who did anything grossly contrary to Bureau rules and regulations and those who were disciplined and thus embarrassed have been suppressed or changed to protect the guilty. Names of places have been changed. Someone may read an anecdote in this book and screech, "That's me! That son of a bitch is talking about me." Don't be too sure. Many of the events described were not one-timers; some are composites.

The reader may find in this account a tendency to emphasize the bizarre and absurd. For better or worse, many characteristics of Bureau life—which some people took very seriously—fell into these categories.

One must also keep in mind that this is a kind of oral history with many of the weaknesses of that form, particularly bias on the part of the narrator. A narrator remembers too many of the wrong things that were done to him and to his friends, and he perhaps gives them a significance they do not deserve. He condemns and criticizes. But it's almost like forgiveness when he goes ahead, tells what he knows or feels, and doesn't let it worry him too much.

I do not feel bitter about my FBI experience. On the whole, it was an interesting place to work. I have but one life and happened to spend a large part of it in the FBI. I just never adopted the Director as my father, which seems to have happened in the case of many other employees.

In the FBI under Mr. Hoover, you had to work on the premise that the Director was infallible. If you did not really believe this—and of course most employees certainly did not—you nevertheless had to pay lip service to it to survive. Anyone who ever worked for the Director and who denies that this condition prevailed is either mentally retarded or lying. And, if you were ambitious and desired to rise in the organization, you had to pay a still higher toll in the form of exaggerated sycophantic respect and adulation for him.

As he grew older, the Director became more and more prone to stereotype all employee dissenters along the lines of Bob Haldeman's magic acronym, DED: "Dissent Equals Disloyalty." When outsiders criticized him, he stigmatized them with such labels as "pinko gadflies," "pseudo-intellectuals," and "liberal eggheads." His characteristic response to criticism was to counterattack the critic rather than to determine if any of the charges were justified. In his entire life as a public servant I do not recall an instance in which he ever publicly admitted he was wrong about anything.

Ralph de Toledano, a journalist who knew Hoover for years and admired him, does say in his book *J. Edgar Hoover: The Man in His Time* that Hoover once admitted having been conned twice in his life—once by a door-to-door salesman who sold him black sawdust for his flower bed as pure manure, and once by the Birdman of Alcatraz, who sold him a sparrow dyed yellow as a canary.

The following timeworn story may sound like just another weird personal obsession, but it has significance as a Bureau allegory:

Some time ago a girl moved from New York to California because she was afraid of alligators. For several years while living in New York she had noticed newspaper and magazine advertisements offering baby alligators for sale in Florida. The ads said they could be shipped anywhere on request. She occasionally entertained the thought of sending one as a present to someone she did not like as a practical joke.

One evening while having a drink with an ecologist friend she mentioned the alligator ads and said what fun it would be to send one unexpectedly to someone. The ecologist, a very serious young man, then told her the story that drove her from New York.

The ecologist said that so many practical jokers had shipped baby alligators to friends in New York they were becoming a menace. Most of the recipients immediately flushed them down the commode and thought they were rid of them for good. Well, they were wrong, he said. A hell of a lot of those alligators had survived and grown to great size in the sewers beneath the city.

"I predict," the ecologist said, "the day will come when there will be so many alligators in the sewers that they will burst forth—leaping at people from manholes in the streets, swimming ashore from the Hudson and East Rivers, and even attacking the Battery and crawling up Wall Street. Many of the strong smaller ones will probably crawl back up the pipes down which they were flushed and emerge from the commodes of their former owners, seeking vengeance."

This was the most unnerving statement the girl had ever heard. She entered her bathroom that night apprehensively and used the facilities with great care, fearful that a previous tenant may have flushed away a baby alligator which was now ready to return for revenge. Her apprehension increased over the following weeks to such a degree that her analyst advised her to move to California, where the Pacific waters were supposed to be too cold for alligators. She followed his advice.

Bureau people occasionally tried to dispose of their problems as they would of baby alligators, and sometimes the problems crawled back up the pipes to haunt them. Mr. Hoover was no exception. During his long reign as Director he flushed many an unwanted employee down the drain, and a few tenacious ones crawled back to nip at his backside. Some wrote books holding up his faults, real and imagined, to public scrutiny. Others leaked stories to the press about his less admirable qualities and even wrote their senators about his more grievous outrages against personnel.

But he fought them all, using DED, the magic acronym, and most of his detractors learned how useless it was to question a living legend about his actions, even when they had the goods on him, because he was so expert at clouding his answers in the mythology that he had created for his institution and that most of the public accepted without question.

As far as employees were concerned his Directorship was a stormy quest for creative conformity. Many of us went with him on the quest, partway or all the way, but then often became bored and infuriated and wanted to quit. Scores did quit and found easier ways of making a living. I heard the head of another government agency once say, "He has run off more good personnel than most agencies ever see." Some of us could not quit. We put on the armor and strapped on the sword and kept them on until we were mustered out after the campaigns were over and he told us we could go home.

There has been a lot of phony stuff written about the FBI, for example, the recent "FBI" television series. Just as Patrick V. Murphy, former New York Police Commissioner, laughs in discomfiture at the "Lieutenant Kojak" image of the New York detective, I laugh with the same discomfiture as the "Inspector Erskine" image of an FBI agent, especially an FBI inspector. The only trouble-shooting inspectors in the Hoover FBI when I was in it were those who shot trouble at employees who wrote anonymous letters to the Director complaining about unhappy working conditions or who had committed acts of personal misconduct which might "embarrass" the Bureau. The Inspector Erskine hero, engaging in his personal war against crime, is the epitome of unreality, a creature of the electronic media and the FBI Crime Records Section.

You might say that as an FBI special agent I was always irreverent, confused, undermotivated, going nowhere in particular, with little on my mind except survival. Cynicism is probably the best word to describe my attitude toward the Bureau then and now. Some scholars list cynicism as one of the most common individual reactions to frustrations arising from institutional pressures. The bureaucratic institution is a blind organism that ignores individuals, they say, and cynicism is a defense mechanism. The FBI under J. Edgar Hoover was a unique institution. It was a highly personalized, one-man institution, somewhat similar historically to the old Ford Motor Company when Henry the Elder *was* the company. J. Edgar Hoover *was* the FBI. And he was not a blind organism. He and his "personal representatives" stared hard at their employees with the unwinking, all-seeing eye of the Cyclops to detect manifestations of disloyalty and complacency.

Death took him in May 1972, saving him the ignominy of being replaced as Director by a lesser mortal. There was no way it could have been done gracefully, as far as he was concerned. Removal from *his* office under any circumstances would have been the act of an enemy. To his way of thinking, there was simply no one else in the world fit to replace him and never would be.

In its days of glory, Mr. Hoover's FBI was a tight little world that danced to the tune of his strident trumpet blasts from the heights of Olympus. Olympus was Washington, D.C., where the Director had been born January 1, 1895, and lived all his life. As I have said, Washington was known in the Bureau as SOG, the Seat of Government. SOG was a mountaintop shrouded in a dung-colored cloud of mystique. The rest of the United States and its possessions was the Field, a vast fief held by Mr. Hoover in his capacity as Director of the FBI.

The Field, from the viewpoint of Mr. Hoover and his minions at SOG, was an area of disorder made up of field offices peopled by Special Agents in Charge (SACs), Assistant Special Agents in Charge (ASACs), field supervisors, and lowly special agents on the bricks, some with fingernails bitten down to the nubs, manning the field offices and resident agencies, constantly trying to create the illusion for SOG that everything was in order and being run according to the Director's master plan. Of course the Director was not deceived. He knew there were weaklings and malingerers out there, flouting his rules and goofing off. Periodically he sent forth raiding parties to attack field offices and tear them apart in search of heresy and disloyalty. He called these depredations office inspections. They resembled the cornfield scene in *Planet of the Apes*—when the apes came galloping through on their horses lassoing all the humans in sight. In the Bureau the apes were called inspectors, or in Bureau vernacular, "goons."

What the Field people knew, and Mr. Hoover apparently did not, was that following all the rules all the time would have meant self-destruction. Had all the nutty rules, orders, and instructions been carried out to the letter simultaneously, the organization would have collapsed from internal explosions like those funny cars the clowns used to drive at circuses.

On the other hand, maybe the Director's master plan

was to submerge the Field in so many rules and regulations that all of them could not possibly be adhered to. All of his employees would be chronically guilty of breaking some rule or other and thus constantly eligible for disciplinary action if the Director saw fit to dish it out.

The Director was especially alert for flaws in the character of the SACs and their assistants, the ASACs. He constantly reminded them that they were his "personal representatives" and that they must not "coddle" the agents. Two of the many fatal ways that SACs and ASACs could err in the eyes of the Director were (1) by building private empires in their field divisions, that is, acting independently of SOG, and (2) by becoming complacent, that is, not welcoming transfers to larger offices when openings occurred.

The worst of the Field lot, in the Director's opinion, were resident agents, agents who were allowed to reside outside the enclaves of the headquarters cities and thus arrange their lives and work with a minimum of supervision. Mr. Hoover called resident agents necessary evils. "If they are not dedicated men, they have the greatest sinecures in the world," he said.

As the Director grew older, he isolated himself at SOG issuing orders and directives in the form of "SAC Letters," constantly adding to the vast laundry list of thou-shalt-not actions, which, if committed by a Bureau employee, meant punishment. His was the voice from the burning bush, meting out sentences—delays of pay raises, reductions in grade, transfers to Siberia-like field offices presided over by Neanderthal SACs, discharge "with prejudice"—all with no recourse, no appeal, no hope of mercy. He was old-fashioned, and so were his punishments. They were reminiscent of the eighteenth-century English law, which provided public hangings for thieves and pickpockets. While the hangings were carried out, other thieves and pickpockets, undeterred by the executions, worked busily in the crowd. Mr. Hoover's punishments were about as effective. While some victim in a field office was being led to the gallows by the inspectors for breaking a rule, almost everyone else went on about his business of breaking rules and hoping he would not be caught.

It may sound a little crazy, but for us non-nailbiters this danger of disciplinary action was what made Bureau service exciting. The game was to break or bend the rules without getting caught. Most of us who survived for years in the Field became, by necessity, expert players. Of course, occasionally someone lost and a thunderbolt from SOG landed with a crash on his head. Those nearby who emerged from the smoke unscathed would shudder with relief and marvel at the degree of overkill.

The Field people were not the only ones to tremble when the thunderbolt landed. Assistant directors, inspectors, and other SOG officials could also be busted. To protect themselves, they constantly had to prove their devotion to him by improving on his orders, making them more strict and the penalties more and more severe, even when their own peers were concerned.

On one occasion at SOG, just prior to dismissing one of his executive conferences of high-ranking Bureau officials, Mr. Hoover said suddenly, "I have been looking over the supervisors at the Seat of Government. A lot of them are clods. Get rid of them." Then he disappeared into his inner office. That statement led to the formation of an investigative panel to identify and expel the clods. The panel became known in Bureau history as the Clod Squad.

Of course no one dared ask the Director to identify any of the clods or to elaborate on his observation in any way. That might have proved fatal to the career of the questioner. So the Clod Squad concentrated on finding supervisors with traits known to be despised by the Director, especially complacency, that cowardly lack of burning desire to ascend in the Bureau. The most common mark of the complacent SOG supervisor was his yearning to stay where he was, in the same job he had held for years, hiding in a cubbyhole. The really courageous and noncloddish supervisors burned with the desire to return to the Field as SACs and ASACs and lash their unwashed mobs into submission so they could be lassoed by the apes galloping through the cornfield. The problem was that most of the Clod Squad members, SOG supervisors of long standing, fell into the complacent category. They were themselves clods under their own definition. They did not want to return to such primitive frontier posts in the Field as Memphis, Omaha, or Little Rock. They had built snug nests in Silver Spring, Rockville, Alexandria, and Falls Church, and had joined country clubs where they played golf and bridge. They had found a home at SOG. But now they had to produce some sacrificial clods to satisfy the Director until he found another project to occupy his mind.

One former clod told me, "They would call you in and ask all sorts of questions about why you hadn't asked for transfer to the goons or for promotion to ASAC. They asked me, 'Why haven't you asked to be a New Agents counselor?' Nobody in his right mind would volunteer for that job, but of course I couldn't say that. 'I just haven't gotten around to it yet,' I said. After the interview I went to a member of the squad who was a supervisor in the Administrative Division, a clod if there ever was one. I told him confidentially he could identify me as a clod if he would get me a transfer to a field office near my home. He worked it out with the other mem-

bers. They made it sound like a disciplinary transfer and
the Director went for it. I didn't give a damn. Me and
the squad were both satisfied. I got a transfer home and
they got credit for identifying a clod."

Then there was the case of a cloddish friend of mine,
Homer Goldthwaite. He had been at SOG for years as
a supervisor in a section called Name Check. Guess what
they did in Name Check. Right. They checked names.
The main qualification for working there was a pro-
ficiency with the alphabet. The Clod Squad called in
Homer and asked him if he were ambitious. He said hell
yes. And they asked him if he thought he had brains
enough to run a field office. He said absolutely. They
asked what he thought his strong points were as an
administrator. He gave them a long list. Homer had
decided that if he could sell them on the idea he really
was ambitious then they would keep him at SOG just to
frustrate him.

Finally someone asked him a snide question. "You
have given us a long list of your strong points. What do
you consider your weakest point?"

Homer thought that over for a while. He had not
been prepared for that type of back-stabbing question.
He finally said, "My handwriting. I guess that's my
weakest point."

"Your handwriting? How about explaining that?
What's weak about it? Your spelling?"

"Oh, no," said Homer, "I spell very well. I'm in Name
Check. If I couldn't spell—"

"Well, what in the hell is wrong with your handwriting?"

"It's like this. I get to work very early every morning.
I'm an early riser. I seem to think more clearly in the
morning. So when I'm in my office about 6:30 A.M. or
so, I write out all sorts of notes for suggestions to im-

prove our operations in Name Check, suggestions to be discussed at our section meeting at 2 P.M. every day. The problem is that by the time afternoon comes, my handwriting has gotten cold and I can't read it. I've got all those notes written out but I can't read them. That's why I say my weakest point is my handwriting."

There was silence for a while from the Clod Squad. Finally the chairman said, "Get out."

"Now, you can see that was a very ambiguous order," said Homer, "an order subject to several interpretations. It could have meant 'get out of the Bureau.' It could have meant 'get out of SOG and return to the Field.' Or it could have meant simply 'get out of this room and return to Name Check.' I gave it the last interpretation and went back to Name Check and took up where I left off. Nobody's bothered me since. I know Name Check's not a very glamorous assignment. Nothing very exciting ever happens there, except when a name comes in misspelled. But I'll bet old Junior Zimbalist Erskine couldn't do it. I'd like to see the Clod Squad get a hold of him."

So a zany, antic war went on constantly and grew wilder as time went by. As you read on about the war, about the games people played to survive, and about some of the casualties, it may seem that the actions of many of the people who rose to high rank in the Bureau were irrational. It's true, they were. Did not Lord Keynes say, "There is nothing so disastrous as a rational policy in an irrational world"? This leads logically to the formula for success in the Bureau: I = R, Irrationality equals Rationality.

In addition to the war and the games and the casualties, this book is also about Mr. Hoover himself—a living legend, a sacred cow, a dinosaur in the nation's backyard who could gobble you up if you didn't look out.

2

The Blindfolded Chimpanzee Called Fate

Some of my so-called friends, especially those who act out their roles on the academic scene, have asked me, "How in the hell did a nut like you ever get into the FBI in the first place and how in the hell, after getting in, did you manage to stay so long?" I've asked myself that question. The best answer I can give is that I sort of wandered into the Bureau in 1948, hung around for twenty-three years, and then wandered out again. Now I'm wandering around out here in the world.

I went on active duty as an army reservist at Fort Hood, Texas, during the summer of 1948. I did not do this because I liked army life. I did it because I needed the money and there weren't a lot of jobs to be had just then. I spent most of that summer soldiering and waiting for a committee to approve my master's thesis at the University of Texas. We summer soldiers were veterans of World War II, assigned to administering two-week training cycles to other reservists. There wasn't much to do in the way of entertainment at Fort Hood. We played bingo at the service clubs, drank beer at the PX, and went to the movies every time the feature changed at the base theater.

One of the movies I saw that summer was an FBI movie, *The Street with No Name*. I don't remember much about it except that two of the actors in the cast were Mark Stevens and Lloyd Nolan and I can remember a pontifical voice, at the beginning or end, intoning something like, "J. Edgar Hoover, Director of the Federal Bureau of Investigation, has called the street of crime in America the street with no name. It can be the street of a large metropolis. It can be Main Street in your own home town." Well, I thought, that sounds pretty good. J. Edgar Hoover must be a pretty sharp phrasemaker to dream up a title like *The Street with No Name*. That was before I learned about Crime Records, the Bureau's name for its public relations department, where many of Mr. Hoover's sharp quotations were manufactured.

After my thesis was accepted and I finished my soldiering, I ventured into the world to seek employment and found that a Master of Arts degree in English was a fragile shield to ward off the assaults of a predatory economy, especially in Texas.

"The all bidness doesn't give a shit about Beowulf," one personnel interviewer from a major oil company informed me.

In desperation I applied for a job as a clerk in the FBI headquarters in Washington. Some time later I received a telegram notifying me I had received the appointment. This telegram was signed "J. Edgar Hoover" and requested that I not give any publicity to the matter. "This must be a big deal," I thought to myself. "Maybe he has a confidential mission in mind for me." I got on the next train for Washington.

My first day I reported late for work at the Justice

Building at Ninth and Pennsylvania. I arrived at least half an hour after the specified time, 9 A.M. I had attended a party given by some Georgetown students the night before and had overslept. I knew better than to own up. One thing I had learned in the army was never, never admit anything resembling a mistake or oversight. I told the supervisor who greeted me with a frown that I had caught the wrong bus that morning. I told him I was a country boy from Texas, not used to big cities, who got lost easily on buses and streetcars. I didn't mention I had never gotten lost on buses and streetcars in Dallas, Chicago, New York, London, Paris, Marseilles, or Munich. He grudgingly accepted my excuse. He seemed pleased that I had already found a place to live— a subterranean room next to the furnace in a red brick row house on O Street Northwest at $8 a week—but said I had better get used to getting to work on time because the Bureau was very strict about that. The Bureau, he said, maintained *registers* that you signed in on when you came to work and signed out on when you left. According to him, these registers were extremely important. I said I would do my best to be on time in the future. He said "my best" had better mean I got to work on time or I wouldn't last long. After that veiled threat, he led me through the routine business of signing several registers and having my picture taken for my identification tag.

I was assigned to the Records and Communications section in the Justice Building and spent my days filing large stacks of mail into bound folders. Since I attended college in the morning, my working hours were from 1 P.M. until 10 P.M., with an hour off for dinner at six. When I returned after dinner I generally spent my evenings "chasing" files for the night supervisor and for other supervisors working late.

I was amazed at the difference between the Bureau by day and the Bureau by night. During the day the Director and all the assistant directors were there, and the halls, offices, and filing areas teemed with supervisors and clerks. About 5 P.M. Miles, the night supervisor, appeared, carrying his black metal lunch box. As a rule, the place was almost completely cleared out by 8 P.M., and then Miles ran the whole show practically single-handed. He read all the incoming teletypes, answered them, and talked on the telephone to field offices all over the United States. There were bank robberies in Knoxville and extortion cases in Miami and kidnapings in Phoenix and Los Angeles. He handled them all, counseling nervous SACs and occasionally checking his decisions by calling SOG officials at home. I sometimes hung around his office until after midnight, just talking.

"Goddam, don't you have a home?" he would say. But he seemed to enjoy company on quiet nights. He knew about Beowulf and had even heard of Grendel and Grendel's mother. "Don't tell anybody. The inspectors might think I'm queer or something. I want to stay in Washington for a while."

Miles had been at SOG almost two years, but during his first five years in the Bureau he had been transferred to seven different field offices.

"Who decides where they are going to send you and why?" I asked.

"If you could find that out, you would solve one of the major mysteries of this outfit. Maybe there's a monkey up there who throws darts at a map of the U.S. If you ever find out the truth of the matter, you let me know, will you?"

By the next night I had it figured out by intuition and induction. "It's a blindfolded chimpanzee," I said to Miles. "He sits on a desk in the Administrative Division.

The Director hands him a dart with an agent's name on it and the ape throws it blindfolded at a large map of the United States. The agent goes to the field office nearest the spot the dart strikes. After each throw, the Director rewards him with an oreo cookie."

"Why does an agent sometimes actually get his office of preference? Just luck?"

I was ready for that. "Mostly it's just luck, but sometimes the Director lets the ape lift the blindfold a little and peek. The ape is really an expert dart thrower. He can hit any office he wants to if the Director tells him which one, and he's allowed to peek."

"How does the Director reward him for that?"

"He gives him a piece of lime pie from that restaurant in Miami Beach where he likes to eat."

"Who told you about the restaurant and the lime pie?"

"The clerk who helps the supervisor who keeps track of the Director's favorite food and eating places. He's the clerk who types up all the recipes for the Director's favorite dishes. Every time the Director tells Miss Gandy he likes something, she tells the supervisor and he has to get the recipe. The clerk said that just a few weeks ago the SAC at Miami sent an agent to SOG on an airplane carrying one of the Director's favorite lime pies in his lap."

"Tell that clerk he better stop running off at the mouth or the Director will hit him in the face with a pie."

"O.K.," I said, "but it all sounds kind of funny."

"Well, it's not so damn funny, and neither is that ape of yours. But just between us, what's the ape's name?"

"His name is Fate," I said.

Miles thought about that for a while. Having just finished his supper from a lunch box, he lit a big cigar. "You know, Joe, I was SAC of an office for a while before I came up here to take over this big deal. I have seen characters like you before. Most of them are in resident agencies, towns outside headquarters city. You undoubtedly have the mentality and outlook of a resident agent."

"Is that good?"

"No," he said. "The Bureau—even the Director—finds resident agents hard to cope with."

"I may have to transfer to the State Department to find people who understand me," I said.

"You do and you may lose your cherry in the men's room, too," he said. "And keep one thing in mind, seriously. You don't *transfer* out of the Bureau anywhere. You either resign, retire, or get kicked out. You don't transfer."

I was to find this out for myself later.

The work was dull. Clerks ran all over the place with files, carrying them by the armful or pushing them in carts from place to place. Most of them were boys and girls just out of high school, recruited from rural areas, where they had been sold on the glamour of working for the FBI, for very low pay. At twenty-seven I was older than most clerks, and since I always wore a suit and tie they would often mistake me for a supervisor. When I walked through a filing unit where the clerks did not know me, the kids would stop giggling and goofing off and start filing mail furiously. I would frown at them as I went by, as I had seen the real supervisors do. The effect was generally the same, a sort of hangdog, what-have-I-done-wrong-now? response. Guilt hung heavy over the clerical and supervisory world at SOG. Once I met a young agent supervisor walking along an aisle and frowned at him. He scuttled away nervously. I swaggered with pride after that. An accusing frown went a long way, if you got yours in first.

All the clerks had a daily quota of mail to file. Some

would file theirs fast and then goof off. The male clerks stood around in the rest room gossiping and smoking, talking about how it would be when they became agents. Practically all of them wanted to become special agents, and many of them did. When I first went to SOG I thought that agents' classes were limited to law graduates and accountants. I found out this was not so. The Director could appoint anyone he pleased. He had made several of his black chauffeurs agents, and they did not even have to go through the Academy. I was surprised to learn that a Bureau clerk with a few years of work experience could qualify for agents' class merely by completing one of the "quickie" accounting courses offered by Washington business colleges of the nonacademic variety.

Bureau clerks were encouraged to be suspicious of one another and report any questionable activities. This led to some tattling and snitching among the clerks, incited by personnel supervisors who developed stool pigeons to keep up with what was going on. The Bureau seemed to take a lot of interest in the sexual activities of the clerks. Allegations of s-e-x activities could get a clerk fired faster than almost anything. Of course, when a clerk did report something on another clerk, it was a hot potato that had to be tossed upward until the potato reached the top, where most doubts regarding dubious conduct were resolved by dismissing the accused clerk.

I asked Miles once why there was so much interest in the employees' sex activities.

"Somebody up there don't screw anybody but agents any more," he said obscurely.

During the spring of 1949 I felt I was on a slow ferry to nowhere. I was not enjoying the urbanized atmosphere of the Washington university I attended or the anxiety-ridden halls and offices of the Justice Building. I certainly was not making any money. After deductions my net pay was thirty-five dollars a week, from which I had to pay eight dollars for room rent, leaving twenty-seven dollars to squander on food, clothing, and entertainment.

I was sitting on a stool in the Men's Bar at the Willard Hotel one payday night, nursing a beer, when a man hit me on the back and called me a son of a bitch. It was my old battalion commander from the ETO, and he was in a happy, drink-buying mood, having just been appointed an assistant to the chief of civilian personnel in the Department of Defense. When he heard about my starvation wages, he took me to dinner and offered me a job in his section at Defense at a salary almost double what the Bureau was paying me. The job would not be open until the new fiscal year began on July 1, he said. Since it was then March, I had plenty of time to get my application in. He gave me his card with his Pentagon address. "Fill out the standard government application blank," he said, "and mail it to me personally. Us guys from the old 19th AIB have to stick together, don't we?"

"Hell, yes," I said.

I filled out the form and mailed it to him. A few days later he responded with a cordial note saying he had received the application and was putting it in the mill. I presumed I would be hearing from him or the Defense Department sometime in the future.

A couple of weeks later, I was ushered into the office of a supervisor in the Administrative Division. He motioned me to a chair, closed the door, sat down behind his desk, and looked at me with an expression of reproachful sorrow. "Aren't you happy here, Schott?"

"I'm fairly happy, I guess," I said. "But the work's dull and the pay is low."

"Is that your excuse for submitting this?" He dropped

23

the application blank that I had mailed to my friend in the Defense Department in front of me as though it was something nasty.

I told him about meeting my former battalion commander and his offering me the job.

"Why didn't you inform the Bureau of your action?"

"It never even crossed my mind," I said. "I considered it a personal matter. If I do get the job, it won't start until July first. I intend to give the Bureau thirty days notice if that happens."

"Didn't you know that the Defense Department would send this through for an agency check and we would find out about it?"

"I didn't know what they would do with it. And I have no objection to your finding out about it. What's wrong with applying for a job that pays almost double the salary of my job here?"

"Schott, you don't have just a job, here. You are an employee of the FBI—"

"—in a job that pays $2,400 a year," I finished for him. "The job at the Defense Department pays over $4,500 a year. It's a research and report-writing job. My job here is just pulling files. I would be stupid to turn that down."

"Don't you know it's against the rules to apply for another government job while you are on duty with the FBI?"

"What? I never heard of that rule. Where is it?"

"It's against the rules for an employee to use his present official position with the FBI to seek employment elsewhere."

"I don't have any official position with the FBI," I said. "I'm just a clerk making $2,400 a year. You don't for a minute think, do you, that the man at Defense is offering me a job there because I'm an FBI clerk?"

"I don't doubt it at all. Someone at the Department of Defense may be trying to recruit our people to find out what we're doing over here."

"Well, I don't know what they would expect to find out from me. All I do is chase files for supervisors and file mail. I don't have any inside information that would help anybody."

"You may know more than you think," he said mysteriously.

I sat there trying to think about what I might know that anyone would be interested in and couldn't think of anything. "He's offering me a job," I said, "because we served together in the same outfit during the war. He was my commanding—"

"You are still on probation, you know," he said. "If you are not happy here, we may have to terminate you administratively."

"For what reason?"

"For disloyalty," he said.

"Disloyalty?" I was surprised. "Look, I served in the Army four years and have the Bronze Star and a Purple Heart. What kind of disloyalty are you talking about?"

"Disloyalty to the Director," he said. "Going behind his back to another agency and trying to get a job after he has entrusted you with an appointment."

I thought it over for a minute. "That leaves me with just one alternative."

"What's that?"

"I'll go in and talk to the Director and tell him you've accused me of disloyalty and explain to him why I made application to another agency. That I simply need more money to live on."

The supervisor squirmed about in his chair. He didn't relish the thought of my going in to see the Director, that was plain. "You might get in more trouble than you are in already if you do that," he said. "You can't predict how the Director may react."

"I'm not in any trouble," I said. "It's as simple as night and day. I've got a low-paying job here, and there's a higher-paying job over at Defense. That's all there is to it. I'm ambitious. I want a better job."

"Have you ever applied for New Agents class?"

"No. I thought you had to be a lawyer or an accountant," I said.

"There are exceptions," he said. "Occasionally."

"Could I be an exception?" I asked.

"You might, provided you cancel this," he nodded at the Defense Department application. "You cancel that and then fill out this." He handed me an application for the position of special agent. "Then we shall see what we shall see."

"In other words," I said, "I cancel out on the Defense job but I still don't have any assurance whatsoever on the agent job. I'm out on a limb."

"It's a calculated risk," he admitted. "You may screw up on one of the interviews or tests. You seem to have a lot of far-out ideas. But if you're accepted, it will pay more than the Defense job. In any case, if you go in to see the Director and he dismisses you during your probationary period 'with prejudice' as a result of your making an application to another agency, you might very well be disqualified permanently from getting a government job anywhere."

I picked up the agent application. "I'll have to think it over," I said.

"You have until tomorrow," he said. "I can't sit on the Defense application any longer than that. There's a deadline on it."

"Okay," I said. There was always a deadline in the Bureau. "I'll let you know tomorrow."

3

"It's a 'We' Organization, Me and Clyde"

My strongest recollection of that winter and spring in Washington when I was a clerk is the atmosphere of anxiety and fear that pervaded the halls and offices of the FBI. You could see it in the faces of the small-fry Bureau supervisors hunched over desks in crowded offices, grimly pawing through stacks of brown-backed files trying to meet deadlines, and in the faces of the furtive clerks scurrying down the halls. The atmosphere most affected the young, impressionable clerks. Either they became depressed to the point where they soon resigned, or they learned to accept anxiety and dread as natural parts of their environment. The most dedicated Bureau employees I have ever known were former clerks who came in young and embraced early the concept of the Director's omnipotence. I learned very soon that these people could be dangerous. Some of them were ignorant and some were smart, but most of them were so proud of their status as FBI employees that they felt they must report any word or deed indicating disloyalty to the Director.

Manifestations of loyalty were numerous. During my era as a clerk the assistant director who handled public relations for the Bureau was a big, dark man called "Nick the Greek" by the clerks and supervisors. Like most of the truly dedicated men of the inner circle he demonstrated his dedication to the Director by spending long hours in the office and creating the appearance of working himself to death. Occasionally he would fall out of his chair with a crash. The assistant director was a large man, so the crash was always loud enough to attract witnesses: clerks, stenographers, and underlings who enjoyed the show as a break in dull routine. The FBI nurse always hurried in with the smelling salts and soon had the Greek propped up at his desk again, flailing away at his papers.

On one occasion the Washington *Post*, that long time critic of the Director and his Bureau, printed a story especially disturbing to the Director. The *Post* printed so many stories that disturbed him it would probably be impossible to identify the particular one at this late date. Whatever it was, the story was printed, and the Director summoned Nick the Greek. Since the *Post* editor was beyond his reach, the Director attacked the Greek for failure to prevent its appearance, as though he had some control over it.

"Mr. Hoover," Nick the Greek allegedly said, "If I had known that they were going to print those subversive, Communist-inspired lies about you, I would have gone over there and hurled myself bodily into the presses."

That answer, according to the grapevine, pleased and even amused the Director. "Nick may not be very smart, but nobody can doubt his loyalty," he is supposed to have said.

The only chair-fallout I ever observed at SOG was performed by Kit Collins, who was chief of the Special Inquiry section. The Collins incident was more of a chair-slideout than a fallout. I don't believe he faked it, although Collins was definitely a supervisor with martyr tendencies.

After I surrendered to the supervisory troll in the Administrative Division by canceling my application to the Defense Department and submitting one for appointment as a special agent, I began doing a lot of file-chasing for supervisors of the Special Inquiry section. Most of the special inquiries came from the White House and were considered "hot" because they had short deadlines. They were expedited to the point of hysteria. A hundred or so supervisors were jammed into the offices of the Special Inquiry section, and from dawn until dusk they sat behind piles of files trying to compose, from information in the various files, memoranda on the individuals inquired about. Many of the names came in without sufficient identifying data, and sometimes the inquiries were duplicated—two or more requests would come in on the same person—in which case two or more supervisors would be simultaneously doing the same work and fighting each other for the same files. Even when different individuals were involved, so many of the names being searched appeared in the same files that it was not unusual for several supervisors to need the same ones at the same time. They continually hid them from each other, because each was worried about his own deadlines and no one else's. I brought files in by the cartload and took them back when the supervisors finished with them. I also had to try and keep track of who had which files and referee fights between supervisors who wanted the same ones at the same time.

Extra desks had been jammed into the rooms, and everyone fought his private deadline battle behind his file stacks, snarling viciously at anyone who tried to remove any from his desk. The reviewers thumbed through the volumes and mumbled into dictaphones, transferring the bones from one graveyard to another, so to speak. On those rare days when there were only a few names coming in, the reviewers hid behind their stacks and read newspapers. To read a newspaper at SOG, unless it was some assigned task like reading the *Daily Worker* for Communist Party intelligence or reading the New York and Washington newspapers for derogatory or laudatory references to the Director, was a punishable offense. But the supervisors were so isolated behind their files that on one occasion one died and no one else in the room knew it for a long time. He just put his head down on his desk and never lifted it up again under his own power. A friend came by at lunch time to see if he was ready to go across the street for a sandwich and found him face down on his desk, dead from a heart attack. He had been dead for more than two hours. His passing had gone unnoticed because the others were so busy pumping paper to the White House. They shipped his body back to Indiana or wherever he came from, and the Director wrote a letter to his widow praising her late husband's dedicated service, assuring her that he had died gloriously in the service of his country.

"If I die fighting for my country behind this stack of files, don't send my body back to Iowa," one of the supervisors told the harassed, tremulous Kit Collins. "Just stuff my body into a filing cabinet and tell the Director I died game and to resurrect me when he needs me."

When anyone said anything disrespectful like that about the Director, Collins always ran off to his tiny cubbyhole office and hid. The Director's ears were everywhere. Disrespect was disloyalty, and disloyalty, and the toleration of disloyalty, were punishable. Collins had spent almost twenty years in the Bureau, most of the time at SOG squirreling around among the files, digging out stuff on applicants and the Director's friends and enemies and writing memos. He was prematurely white-haired. Not just gray, but white. When the phone on his desk rang, he always jumped and often dropped the receiver before he could get it to his ear, giving the caller an ear-shattering clatter.

"Kit has combat fatigue, no question about it," Miles, the night supervisor, used to say. "He's got the worst case of shell shock I ever saw. But, my God, is he dedicated! You never hear him complain or say anything cross. If the Director told him to eat a pound of horse shit, he'd just ask, 'Where's the spoon?' "

One afternoon Collins's dedication was tested severely. Somewhere in the unholy mess of files and lists one of the memos on a White House appointee had been mislaid and submitted too late to meet the deadline. Someone from the White House called Mr. Hoover to bring the matter to his personal attention. Furious, the Director called Collins. When the phone rang Collins grabbed the receiver and dropped it with a crash. This infuriated the Director even more. He gave Collins a blast that went on several minutes. I happened to walk into his office with my file cart while this was in progress. Collins sat there trembling, his normally ruddy face pale as paper, mumbling, "Yes, Mr. Hoover. Yes, Mr. Hoover. Yes, Mr. Hoover." When the tirade finally ended, Collins, holding the receiver with both hands to keep from dropping it, managed to hang it up without a clatter. Then he slid out of his chair onto the floor under his desk. Miles and I pulled him out and laid him on a couch. While Miles dialed the nurse an urgent summons, I took off the stricken man's shoes and loosened his necktie. His eyes were wide open and his lips were moving. I put my ear down to his mouth to find out if he was asking for something. He wasn't asking for anything. He was saying, "Yes, Mr. Hoover. Yes, Mr. Hoover. Yes, Mr. Hoover."

The nurse came in briskly with ammonia sniffers for his nose and damp cloths for his fevered brow. Such occurrences were routine. "He must have been handed a pretty good jolt," she said with professional detachment. She soon had Collins conscious again, and he immediately staggered back to his desk like a dog returning to a rotten bone.

"Goddam!" said Miles. "The dedicated idiot must be trying to commit suicide. Somebody said he never even went out for lunch today. It's after five o'clock already. I'll try to get him to go across the street and eat something."

After a lot of head wagging and stalling, Collins finally agreed. "I'll go if you order me to," he told Miles. "I always follow orders. If the Director calls again for me, you will have to say that you ordered me to go get something to eat."

"O.K., O.K.," said Miles, "anything to keep you from dropping dead on the floor." He raised his hand and made the sign of the cross dramatically like the Pope. "I hereby order you to go eat dinner. You go too, Joe."

"Don't be sacrilegious," said Collins. "We'll be just across the street."

Collins and I got our hats and topcoats, walked across the street to a restaurant opposite the Justice Building on Pennsylvania Avenue, and sat down in a booth. It was the cocktail hour, and the waitresses were serving double martinis in small glass jugs at bargain prices.

"How about a martini, Kit?"

"Oh, I don't know if I better. Let's just split one maybe."

Collins was a well-known nickel-nursing tightwad, but after spending the morning in class and the afternoon in the madhouse across the street I decided I was going to have a martini if I had to buy one for half the tightwad supervisors in the Bureau. "They're on me," I said.

"Oh, you young unmarried guys," said Collins, shaking his head. "You spend money like water. You'll regret it someday when you have a wife and a house full of kids."

When the martinis arrived, he sipped his appreciatively. "What's your ambition in the Bureau, Joe?"

"To go through New Agents and get out of this nuthouse to a field office."

He jumped apprehensively and looked around. "Don't say things like that out loud, Joe. If the Director heard you say something like that, your days would be numbered." He poured the second half of his martini into the glass. "A bright young fella like you could go a long way in the B. by staying at SOG. You might even have my job one day. But you have to learn to curb your tongue. The Director won't tolerate disrespect." He looked around for the waitress. "Two more of the same, sweetheart. A bird can't fly on one wing."

After the waitress brought the second round, or maybe the third, and Kit had been looking off into space in pensive silence for some time, I said, "Maybe we better order some food, huh, Kit?"

"Don't be so goddam impatient, young fella. You young squirts are always so goddam impatient. I'm in charge here. You think you're the Director, getting impatient like that? We're going to have another little drink and then when we goddam well feel like it, we're going to have a leisuree . . . leisurely dinner, and then we're going back across the street, and I'm going to call that old son of a bitch on the phone and demand an apology. After working for that old son of a bitch for nearly twenty years he can't talk to me like that. Like a dog or something. I know where there's some bodies buried that would stink up Washington, if I dug 'em up. I'll tell the cockeyed world!"

By now I was the one looking over my shoulder apprehensively, because Kit was talking loud. The place was beginning to fill up with diners. A lot of people from the Justice Department and the Bureau ate there regularly. "I'll be back in a minute, Kit," I said. "I got to take a leak."

"Yeah, sonny, go on and take a leak," Collins snarled. "Don't squat to pee. Stand up like a man at the urinal. And while you're taking a leak, I'm going to order another round and then both of us are going over there to the fifth floor and tell that old son of a bitch how the cow ate the cabbage or the corn or whatever it was the goddam cow ate. If Tolson sounds off, I'll stack his ass too. He's nothing but a goddam puppet. Just a goddam puppet!"

That name, Tolson, made me quiver.

From the phone booth outside the men's room I called Miles and told him what was going on. "Kit's dedication and loyalty just wore out. He wants to go up on the fifth floor and tell the Director how the cow ate the cabbage, he says."

"Holy shit!" Miles said. "What else is going to happen? Denver has been on the phone about a bank robbery and Cleveland just sent in a teletype about a hundred thousand dollar extortion demand on the governor. The Old Man's still in his office. Sit on him till I can get there. If he comes back over here drunk and gets up on the fifth floor there'll be mass executions before sunrise."

Miles came in a few minutes later. "I got one of the guys to sit in for me for an hour. Told him I had an emergency at home. I'm parked at the curb. We'll get Kit out there and I'll drive him home."

"You'll shit, too, if you eat regular," said Collins. "I'm not ready to go home. I'm going over there on the fifth floor and tell that old son of a—"

Luckily, Miles was large and overpowering, a former college football lineman. With some wrestling and wheedling he soon propelled Collins outside while I paid the check. We had one bad scene before stuffing Collins into the car parked in the loading zone at the curb. Collins stood, weaving on his feet, his hat crushed on the back of his head, snarling at the building across the street, "It's a 'we' organization, Mr. Hoover! Me and Clyde, that's who *we* is. Me and Clyde. Me and the puppet." He thumbed his nose at the Justice Building. I assumed that the "Clyde" he referred to was Clyde A. Tolson, Mr. Hoover's associate director and closest friend.

Just then a black and white police car rolled by slowly, finally stopped, and began to back up.

"Get him in the back seat and sit on him," said Miles. He hurried over to talk to the policeman.

I pushed Collins into the back seat and sat on him. He kept on saying, "It's a 'we' organization, me and Clyde, me and Clyde."

"You better ride along," said Miles after he returned from talking with the cop. "Kit's so crazy he might jump out in front of a truck or something. I told the cop we were agents from the Washington Field Office and we were arresting this guy for impersonating a federal officer. He bought it O.K."

We delivered Collins safely to his home in Alexandria and received for our trouble a good dose of verbal abuse from his wife, who held us responsible for leading her husband astray. Miles drove me back across the bridge to the District, where I could catch a streetcar home. "For God's sake don't noise this around," he said. "The Old Man would stack all our asses if he heard about it."

The next morning Miles was just leaving when I came in about 8 A.M. to study for a while in the law library before class. "Jesus! That Cleveland extortion kept me here all night. Collins came in a while ago and tried to chew me out for roughing him up last night. I told him to kiss my ass," Miles said and departed.

Collins was in the hall when I signed in on the register that afternoon. "Bankers' hours as usual," he said. Anyone who signed in after 7 A.M. was keeping bankers' hours according to Collins. "Let me give you a little advice, young fella, about drinking. It's ruined many a career in this Bureau, so kind of watch it. You had quite a snootfull last night. A word to the wise is sufficient." Just then the phone on his desk rang and he juggled it wildly but did not drop it.

"Yeah, Kit," I said, "I guess I better slow down a little. Maybe I'll take the pledge or something."

He waved at me frantically to leave the room. "Yes, Mr. Tolson," he said. "It won't happen again, I assure you of that. Yes, Mr. Tolson, I've fixed responsibility in the matter and written a memo. Yes, Mr. Tolson."

I tiptoed out of the room and closed the door behind me.

4

"One of Them Is a Pinhead— Get Rid of Him"

When I was going through New Agents training, an FBI assistant director we called Troutmouth summoned me to a private interview because I had made a grade of 85 on a test covering FBI rules and regulations. I don't think I ever learned 85 per cent of the rules and regulations, even later, after accumulating years of service. Anyway, 85 was the lowest acceptable grade on any New Agents test, but I would probably have gotten off with a warning from my counselor except that the sneaky Special Agent in Charge at the FBI Academy in Quantico had checked the sign-out register for three nights preceding the test and discovered that I had signed out for the movies all those nights. The SAC blabbed to the Training Division. Blabbing probably made him feel a little more secure. So Troutmouth, the assistant director in charge of the Training Division, had summoned me for a personal interview at SOG, and my class counselor became hysterical because he had not been the one to find out and blab on me first.

"For God's sake, be careful what you say," the counselor said. "Your whole Bureau career may be at stake. Wear a dark suit. Wear a white shirt. Dress as if you were going in to see the Director."

I carefully knotted a dark blue necktie and put on the jacket of a new dark blue suit, which I had charged at Woodward and Lothrop in Washington the day after I received my appointment as a special agent. My Bureau career might be at stake, but so was the counselor's, and it was his career he was worried about, not mine. If Troutmouth's interview revealed some serious flaw in my character, he would stack the counselor's ass alongside mine for not finding it first and reporting it.

"Maybe he'll tell me where the blindfolded chimp's dart hit," I said. "I may be going to Miami or San Diego."

"Don't talk about that to him," begged the counselor, to whom I'd told my theory. "Leave the monkey out of it."

"A chimpanzee is an ape, not a monkey."

"Oh, my God!" the counselor wrung his hands. "Where do they find people like you? They must have hired you by mail."

After this much time I cannot recall everything Troutmouth said during my interview with him, but I still recall some of the conversation. After he chewed me out —nothing special to a calloused army vet—he said, "Schott, I feel that your attitude toward your work is not serious enough."

His eyes wandered away from me to the window overlooking the sunny courtyard of the Justice Building where clerks and stenographers were sitting around the fountain on lunch break. He was undoubtedly brooding over my shortcomings. His eyes snapped back at me.

"What do you really believe in, Schott, and why are you here?"

That double-barreled question was bothering me, too. I presented a peculiar problem to Troutmouth, mainly because of my educational background. Troutmouth suspected my master's degree in English might be semi-subversive, like sociology or economics. Everyone else in the class had degrees in law or accounting. Many of the former SOG clerks in the class did not have baccalaureate degrees at all, as I have said. I could have told Troutmouth then and there, if I had been completely honest, that the Bureau was just a job to me, not holy orders. And I could have added, I wouldn't *really like* any regular job, so it didn't make a hell of a lot of difference to me what I did as long as the work had its interesting moments. No matter what I did, I always felt as if I should be doing something else. But I knew better than to tell that to Troutmouth. He would have kicked me out. I had never been kicked out of any job in my life, even though I had disliked them all, and did not intend to let that happen now if I could help it.

I looked Troutmouth in the eye and said, "I believe in America and that's why I'm here. I expect you and the Bureau to believe in it too."

Troutmouth sat up straighter as though someone under his chair had inserted a hot ramrod in his anal canal. I had a momentary feeling that I was through. I was going to have to wrap up my new suit and take it back to Woodward and Lothrop. Then he stood up suddenly and stuck out his hand, which meant I was dismissed. "Have no fear, Mr. Schott," he said, "unlike some of our colleagues in the State Department and elsewhere in Washington, we're all true blue here. In the future I suggest you study the night before a test rather than go to a movie. Movies are all right in their place, but life is serious. Make your life a vector, Mr. Schott, a line with force and direction. Make up your mind where you are going, and then go there by the most direct route."

My anxious counselor was waiting for me when I emerged from Troutmouth's office. "Well?" he asked.

"No sweat," I said. "He just told me to quit going to the movies the night before tests."

"That's great," he said, breathing a big sigh. "That's great." His career plan was operational again. "You got off light. Now, like I told you before, you've got to do what I say and quit telling all those damned stories about blindfolded monkeys. You've got to—"

"He did say something I didn't quite understand," I said.

"What was that?"

"Elwyn?" I asked, that was his first name, "Is there something wrong going on in the class?"

"Why do you ask? What do you mean? What did he say?"

"He told me if I heard anyone say anything or saw anyone do anything that I didn't think looked right, he wanted me to come and tell him about it."

"Oh, hell, Joe," Elwyn laughed nervously. "Don't pay any attention to that bullshit. He's just trying to make a stool pigeon out of you. That happens all the time. Don't pay any attention to that."

We walked toward the elevator to go back to the classroom. I was quiet and thoughtful.

"Joe," said Elwyn finally, "what did *you* say when he asked you to do that?"

"I told him that I had the greatest confidence in you, Elwyn. I said if I saw or heard anything wrong I would report it to you and I was sure you would report it to him."

Elwyn clapped me on the shoulder. "Attaboy! When I get to be SAC I want you in my office." Elwyn had his dreams of grandeur. He punched the elevator button. "Did he make any comment about that? Pro or con?"

"He said he considered you a solid man. Those were his words, 'a solid man.' Was that significant?"

"Wow!" he said. "Was that significant? That's the best news I've heard in a long time. Maybe I'll be going out as ASAC before long."

Elwyn had more important problems in the class than me. There were a lot of nagging, worrisome jobs in the Bureau, but being a New Agents counselor was one of the worst. Some of their problems were unbelievably whimsical.

One of the most whimsical I ever heard arose from the presentation of a New Agents class to the Director. In those days it was part of the training ritual of the classes—each thirty to forty strong—to file quickly through the Director's office to be favored with a sharp glance, a brisk handshake, and a nod before being hustled out the other door. Since the individual's time under Directorial scrutiny amounted to only a few seconds, this particular incident illustrates The Man's acute powers of observation and capacity for quick decision. It also illustrates the ability of those around him to improve upon his instructions.

The New Agents, clad in their dark suits, white shirts, and subdued neckties, flitted by in front of the Director, shaking hands and bowing jerkily like marionettes on strings, and hurried on out. The entire class passed before him within a minute or two.

As the last one disappeared through the exit, the Director said to the counselor of the training class, "One of them is a pinhead. Get rid of him!" Then he went into his private office and closed the door behind him.

Of course, the counselor did not dare ask the Director for additional information to identify the pinhead. He dared not ask the Director anything. Instead, he went to the classroom where the New Agents were assembled and addressed them for a time on some pretext or other, peering at each, trying to identify one whose head looked unusually small. He was unsuccessful. Then the solution struck him. He would check their hat sizes. In those days all agents were supposed to wear hats while on duty, and naturally this rule was strictly enforced at SOG. New agents kept their hats in their individual clothing lockers while taking firearms training at the FBI Academy at Quantico. A day or so later, while the class was on the firing range, the counselor and one of his assistants checked the hats in the lockers. They found that the smallest hat size in the class was six and seven-eighths. But the hell of it was, there were *three* members of the class with that size. There was no help for it: All three with sizes six and seven-eighths were fired. Thus the counselor, by improving on instructions, made sure that the Director's pinhead was eliminated.

Luckily I had a very large head, size seven and a half, and was neither too tall nor too short, or too fat or too lean. My voice was in tenor range and I had no irresistible impulses to goose my classmates in the shower, so the moviegoing incident was my only problem in New Agents.

We had several class casualties, however, during the twelve-week course. One of the casualties became a living example of why it was sound policy never to volunteer information to the Bureau about any sort of personal escapade. After a strenuous week at Quantico, this New

Agent spent a weekend in Washington, sleeping late on Saturday morning and then just hanging around enjoying himself. That night, after dinner, he sat in a bar drinking for some time before deciding to go home. He left the bar, pretty tight, with the intention of hailing a cab. A black and white sedan parked at the curb looked like a cab to him. Jerking open the back door, he lunged into the car saying, "Take me to 2018 O Street, Northwest."

What he thought was a cab was a police patrol car. The cops in the front seat got him out, searched him, and found his gold FBI badge. He had not yet been issued credentials. They took him home, let him into his room with his key, stretched him out on the bed, and left.

Next morning he had a vague recollection of having been taken into custody by the police but could not recall how he had gotten home. He worried about it all day Sunday. Had he been taken in and booked or not? What had happened? He knew if he had been fingerprinted the prints would turn up at the FBI Identification Division in a few days. Then they would find out. The first thing Monday morning he reported the incident to the head of the Training Division. The Bureau checked and found no police record had been made of the incident. But, of course, they fired the guy anyway. He had "embarrassed" the Bureau.

I should explain, I suppose, that when I went through New Agents training in 1949 we spent some of our time in the Justice Building and some at the FBI Academy on the Marine Base at Quantico, Virginia, about fifty miles south of Washington. Lectures on federal laws under FBI jurisdiction and FBI rules and regulations were given at both places, but all the firearms training and the practical problems, such as simulated arrests and crime scene investigations, were held at Quantico.

I found the days and nights at the Academy hard to bear. We slept on narrow beds, four to eight in a room, and ate our meals in the Academy dining room. The cuisine was nothing to leave home for. Evenings were dull, dull, dull. We could loll on the beds in the dormitory rooms upstairs or slump in the chairs of the drab lounge on the ground floor, reading such scintillating periodicals as *Readers Digest* and *American Legion Magazine.* We could go to the movies on the base or to downtown Quantico and drink beer. We had to sign out on a register when we left the building in the evening and sign in again when we returned before the 11 P.M. curfew.

Being at present a teacher, I suppose I should comment on the New Agents' curriculum. The firearms training was just bang, bang, bang on the range all day—pistols, shotguns, rifles, and submachine guns—and the practical problems were simulated crime investigations, which included lifting fingerprints, making plaster casts of tire tracks, photography, and so forth, and simulated arrest situations.

The nucleus of the academic curriculum was the Big Manual, the Bible of the FBI. It was called the Big Manual to differentiate it from the Handbook, which I will talk about later.

There were really two Big Manuals: the Manual of Instructions and the Manual of Rules and Regulations. The Manual of Instructions contained a listing of all the violations of federal law, as well as all the other investigative matters under the jurisdiction of the FBI. It cited pertinent parts of the law for each, listed the elements of the crimes in one-two-three order, and outlined suggested procedures to follow in investigating each. These suggested procedures were more than mere suggestions. If an agent screwed up a case in some way and a supervisor or inspector found out that one of the suggested procedures had not been followed, the agent could get into trouble for committing a "substantive" error. A substantive error in the Bureau, commonly called a "sub," was the same as a mortal sin in the Catholic Church. Unforgiven, it led to damnation. A lot of the lectures in New Agents consisted of horror stories about the terrible punishments inflicted on people who committed substantive errors.

The Manual of Rules and Regulations was the Old Testament of the Bureau, laying down rules of personal conduct that were as punitive and unforgiving as the ancient laws of the Hebrews. This manual contained the revealed word of the Director and catalogued most of the mortal subs that could be committed by an FBI agent.

Eric Hoffer, the longshoreman philosopher, has written somewhere that the last grand act of a dying institution is to issue a newly revised, enlarged edition of the policies and procedures manual. According to this definition, the FBI must have been dying for years under the reign of the Director, because the Big Manual was in a constant state of revision and enlargement. Most of the thickness of the Manual of Instructions was caused by the passage of new laws for the FBI to enforce. Most of the thickness of the Manual of Rules and Regulations could be attributed to the corpses of those careers killed for breaking the Director's rules or committing acts that the Director condemned and then turned into additional rules.

When I came on duty as a Special Agent in 1949, the Manual of Instructions was encased in two fairly thick looseleaf ring binders; when I left twenty-two years later the Manual of Instructions had grown to three very thick looseleaf binders. When I came on duty there were about 120 different classifications of investigations. When

I left in 1971 there were more than 180 classifications.

About the time I entered on duty, the Bureau put out a synopsized version of the two manuals called the Handbook, a smaller three-ring binder. This relieved the individual agents of the responsibility of lugging around the cumbersome Big Manual with them. It was a very practical Handbook. Agents consulted it frequently, because the rules forbidding them to do so many things and the "investigative suggestions" were so multifarious that constant perusal was necessary to keep up with changes and stay out of trouble.

In my declining years I have come to realize how strange New Agents class was in many ways. For example, the class lacked any formalized structure. No class officers were elected. No valedictorian was named at the end. No formal graduation exercises were held, and no class picture was ever taken. No diplomas or certificates of completion were ever handed out. Of course, each New Agent had a letter appointing him a Special Agent of the Federal Bureau of Investigation signed by the Director, and near the end of the New Agents training he received a letter designating the office to which he would be transferred. But it has grown on me over the years how strange it was—considering our modern preoccupation with documents of achievement—certificates, diplomas, college degrees, award scrolls, and the like—that no such document was awarded to those who successfully completed New Agents. My own opinion is that it was a planned omission on the part of the Director. He knew that a certain percentage of those who graduated would be terminated in ignominy, and he did not want any of them lugging off prestigious documents to hang on their walls after they had been dismissed in disgrace. It might give the impression he had endorsed them in some way. Along the same lines, when an agent retired, he received no formal document of the "honorable discharge" variety. Mr. Hoover wrote him a letter of some degree of cordiality determined, I suspect, by the degree of respect and affection projected in the agent's letter requesting retirement. This too may have been planned. Retired agents sometimes betrayed the Director by criticizing him. Why should such a Benedict Arnold have a document showing he had honorably retired from the FBI?

On our last day in New Agents class, just prior to our departure to our first offices, we all appeared at the Justice Building dressed to travel, lugging traveling bags and the Bureau briefcases. We had received individual letters assigning us to our offices a few days before. I was being sent to Newark. In 1949 there were at least fifty field offices in the Bureau, including Honolulu and Anchorage. Since Hawaii and Alaska had not achieved statehood at that time, those last two were very small offices, and no one from my class went to either.

Most of the class members groaned when they saw they were going to such places as Chicago, Pittsburgh, and Detroit. A few, with letters for Phoenix, Miami, and San Francisco, were overjoyed.

When Elwyn, the class counselor, heard I was going to Newark, he shook his head. "Somebody in the Administrative Division must have heard your story about the blindfolded chimpanzee with the darts. They gave you a doozie of an office. But if you get tired of Newark, you can always go to Hoboken or Jersey City. They're right next door to each other."

"Newark covers the whole state of New Jersey," I said. "I might get assigned to a resident agency. One of the In Service agents from there said there are some good RAs—Atlantic City, Morristown, Red Bank—"

"Look, Joe, RAs are the lowest form of animal life. Don't get to be an RA. You'll never amount to anything in this outfit if you do."

Troutmouth himself appeared to give us a little farewell message and horror story.

"Gentlemen," he said, "you are now on your way to the Field where you must bend every effort to live up to the grand traditions of this organization and the splendid example set by your Director. You will find the Field to be full of pitfalls and temptations. Some of you will not survive them. Recently in one of our West Coast offices an incident occurred illustrative of such pitfalls. The Special Agent in Charge of the office was being transferred back here to assume a higher post at the Seat of Government. The members of his office decided to honor him with a farewell party. The place chosen for the party— or I should say, the place ill-chosen for the party —was a local nightclub whose owner was on friendly terms with many members of the office. As the party progressed, most of those attending looked upon the wine when the wine was red, gentlemen. In short, they became intoxicated. The climax of the party was the presentation to the Special Agent in Charge of a farewell gift—an elaborate and expensive pen and pencil set. The presentation was made in a unique way. It was brought to him on a satin pillow borne at arm's length by one of the nightclub performers—a young Negress clad only in high-heeled slippers, red slippers, I believe. A nude Negress, gentlemen," said Troutmouth, hissing on the esses as usual. "A nude Negress presented a Special Agent in Charge of the FBI a gift on a satin pillow in front of a large group which included not only Bureau employees but also outsiders. When the news of this event reached the Director, which it did very quickly, by means of an anonymous letter, I was dispatched as the Director's personal representative to investigate the matter. According to all reports there had been at least a hundred Bureau employees at this party, but I could not find a single one—with the exception of the Special Agent in Charge—who would admit having been in the dining room when the nude Negress appeared bearing her satin pillow. Twenty-three of them, I recall, stated they were making a phone call from a pay booth nearby at the time. Gentlemen, there is only one telephone booth anywhere near the ballroom where the presentation occurred. Twenty-three midgets could not have crowded into it. The same applies to the fifty-odd who swore they were in the men's room answering a call of nature at the time. Gentlemen, the men's rest room at that night-club was equipped with the barest essentials—a commode, urinal, and lavatory. The rest room itself—I measured it—was six feet by eight feet. The idea that fifty or more full-grown men had crowded in there on that fateful night was absurd. Needless to say, gentlemen, that Special Agent in Charge is no longer with the Bureau. He betrayed the Director's trust. Many, many of those who attended the party were severely disciplined." Troutmouth paused for dramatic effect. "I am relating to you this sordid story just prior to your departure for the Field as a warning. . . . This is the type of conduct the Director will not tolerate, gentlemen. Remember that every act on your part after you leave here, either at home or in a public place, as long as you are employed by the Bureau, is a direct reflection on this Bureau and its Director."

With that final horror story fresh on our minds we departed for the Field.

5

"Thank You, Mr. Queensland, That Was the Very Best I've Ever Had..."

"All SACs aren't ninety-nine and forty-four one hundredths per cent pure chickenshit but those that aren't like to walk through a hen house on the way to work and track it all over the office. This is a dangerous type of SAC. If you stand still, he will rub it in your face. If you lie down, he will track it up and down the back of your Robert Hall suit. If you start running, he will throw it at you. Those who smile while they do this are the most dangerous of all. They really love chickenshit."

—JUGBUTT QUEENSLAND

Some time ago I read in an obituary from a newspaper that Jeremiah Bartholomew Queensland, FBI 1926–56, had died in a rest home in Orlando, Florida. A dim photograph of the deceased illustrated the article. I examined it under a magnifying glass and recognized a familiar countenance—tub-handle ears, little piggy eyes, a large loose mouth ready to leer or sneer, and a nose that resembled a blob of Silly Putty molded by a re-

tarded five-year-old. No question about it. It was Jugbutt Queensland.

"Queensland is survived by his wife Mildred and four
daughters," the article said. There was also a dim photograph of Mrs. Queensland. I studied that visage under
the glass. It was indeed Mildred the Fourth. Jugbutt had
tried in vain to run her off, the way he had run off the
first three wives, but Mildred had clung to the miserable
hunk of driftwood she had snagged on the sea of life to
the very end. The caption under the photo proved she
had won final revenge. "Jeremiah Bartholomew Queensland," I read with relish. Alive, Jugbutt always signed his
name "J. B. Queensland" and refused to reveal what the
initials stood for. "Initials only," he used to growl irritably. "They don't stand for any names. I don't understand why in the hell I have to keep explaining that."
Now Mildred had exposed that lifelong bit of fiction by
revealing his true names, probably with a great deal of
satisfaction. I would wager that in a cemetery somewhere
in the vicinity of Orlando there is a tombstone inscribed
with large letters, "Jeremiah Bartholomew Queensland,
1895–1970, Former Special Agent FBI." His associates in
the FBI would like to have added the cryptic inscription,
"Thank you, Mr. Queensland, that was the very best I've
ever had."

I met Queensland in the halcyon days, on arrival at
my second office of assignment. When I stepped off the
elevator there were two people waiting. One was a
stocky, red-faced man of sixty with ears like washtub
handles, squinty, piggy eyes, and a nose like a blob of
Silly Putty. "Hold that goddam elevator door, sonny
boy," he said to me. He spoke with such authority that
I instantly complied.

The red-faced man then turned to the tall, skinny
character he was grasping by an elbow. This was a di-

sheveled man of indeterminate age whose pants looked as if they had been peed in in the not too distant past. "I'm gonna tell you this just once, you wino son of a bitch," said the red-faced man. "If you come up here one more time making complaints, I'm going to throw your ass down the stairs."

The skinny character said, "My shenator will be informed of your impertinensh."

The red-faced man positioned his companion directly in front of the elevator door and said to me, "Look out!"

I jumped out of the way.

He then kicked the skinny character in the butt with such violence that the man crashed into the back wall of the elevator and collapsed. "Push the down button," he growled at me and turned and walked away.

I pushed the down button and the victim disappeared for eternity as far as I know. I never saw him again to my knowledge—although I have seen many of his kind since in flophouses and missions and passed out in alleys. I walked down the hall to the FBI office and was surprised to see the man who had assaulted the wino enter there. I followed and saw him disappear through an inner door, which he opened with his own key.

A little white-haired receptionist and switchboard operator sat behind a counter. I showed her my credentials, and she pressed a button unlocking the door so that I could enter and sign the registers.

"Who was that who came in just ahead of me?" I asked.

"That was Mr. Queensland," the lady said.

"Is he an agent?"

"Yes. He has complaint duty today."

"Does he always treat complainants like he did the last one?"

"Yes," she said, "except when he's in a bad humor. Then he makes them scream before he puts them on the elevator."

I went to the SAC's office and looked in the open door. The SAC was talking on the telephone but motioned me to come in and sit down. He was white-haired and as handsome as the successful businessman in an advertisement for expensive Scotch whisky. His abuse of English was impressive: "You should have knew he would screw it up." He waited a minute for an answer and then said impatiently, "All I know is that it hasn't came in yet." Then he hung up. "I can't get them resident agents off their ass," he said.

I would hear the complaint many times in the future, because I became one of them resident agents who wouldn't get off their ass.

After I introduced myself, he said, "Yeah, I was expecting you. You ain't married, right?"

I owned up that I wasn't.

"You're twenty-eight years old. You ain't queer, are you?"

No, I said, I liked girls.

"Well," he said, "Just don't lay no pipe in my office, see? You get one of these stenos knocked up and by God you'll marry her. The Director don't tolerate agents getting stenos knocked up." Then he picked up his telephone again and dialed an extension. When someone answered he said, "Get your ass in here."

The ASAC appeared immediately through a connecting door. He was a short, undistinguished looking man with a furtive air about him.

"This is the second-office agent the Bureau called about," said the SAC. "Make him read all them memos."

"O.K., Boss," said the ASAC.

"And don't forget what I said about not laying no pipe in this office," the SAC said to me as I left. "And read *all* them memos."

"What do you think of the SAC?" the ASAC asked me after we entered his office and closed the door.

"I never worked for a Harvard graduate before," I said, "but I guess we'll get along O.K."

The ASAC pursed his lips disapprovingly. "If there's anything we don't need here it's another smart ass," he said. He had the office memo file brought in from the chief clerk's office and handed it to me. Then he led me to a desk in the big agents' room, a bullpen type of room where the investigative agents did their paper work.

"Sit anywhere," he said.

So I sat anywhere and read all them memos. The only other people in the room were Mr. Queensland and a stenographer. Queensland was dictating, his voice rising and falling like waves on a stormy beach. Occasionally, when carried away by the sheer excitement of his own narrative, he would stride dramatically around his desk waving his arms for emphasis. His secretary, a squatty female creature, took his dictation staring up at him through thick lenses like a hypnotized frog. When he finished and the frog had hopped away, Queensland took out a large handkerchief, blew his nose with a violent honk, coughed horribly, and spat out the open window. "I hope nobody was walking by just then," he said. He lit a cigar and walked over to my desk. "J. B. Queensland," he said, sticking out his hand.

Queensland was an interesting but opinionated talker. With twenty-five years of service, he was a real old-timer. In 1950 there weren't many people around the Bureau who had been on duty that long. In those days few employees had been on duty longer than the late 1930s. But Queensland had been an agent since 1926. He talked about the Matson kidnaping and the Lindbergh kidnaping and the trial of the Nazi saboteurs and other big cases, but mostly he talked about his sex life, his voice booming out with no restraint.

"I had this friend Bill Jones I used to work with in Savannah," he said. "One afternoon him and I picked up a couple of fast numbers in a blind pig out in the sticks and decided to go out into the bushes and get a little poontang. I stopped the car on a narrow country road and took my girl and the back seat of the car out into the bushes and left old Bill and the other girl in the car. I got my girl down on the car seat and screwed the hell out of her. When I got through, she was all sprawled out across the car seat with that faraway look in her eyes and I said, 'Honey when you pull out of it, come on back of the car. I'm going back and have a little snort out of that bottle of moonshine.' When I got back, there was old Bill walking up and down the road shaking his dick, limp as a dish rag, and in the car was his girl with a mad look on her face.

" 'That bastard can't get up a hard,' she says. 'Honey, I said, I can handle your problem!' So I got into the car and screwed the daylights out of her. She really appreciated it. I thought she was going to claw up the upholstery and kick out the windows and the little dials on the dash with her heels, threshing and kicking around like that. When I finally got through, she looked up at me with those baby blue eyes and said, 'Thank you, Mr. Queensland, that was the very best I've ever had. I want to give you my telephone number and if you are ever in this area again, please call me up. But don't bring that other son of a bitch with you!' " He laughed a gurgling, choking, horrible laugh and, when that fit subsided, launched into an anecdote about his relations with his second wife. It seems they had lived for a while in a garage apartment near the railroad tracks in Indianapolis. "I always set the alarm clock for 6:30 A.M., but there was a train that always came by at 6:15 and blew its whistle. Naturally, I'd jump on top of her as soon as I was awake and at exactly 6:30, her and me and the alarm clock all three went off together." This time the laugh developed in such a paroxysm I thought he was going to choke.

"How many times have you been married, Mr. Queensland?"

"Four," he said sourly. "I managed to shake loose from the first three but this last one is a leech. She says the preacher said 'until death do us part,' and that's how it's going to be. The last time I tried to divorce her, she wrote the Director and told him she was going to cross-file against me and charge adultery. He hauled me in and said, 'Queensland, if she proves adultery against you, I'll fire you with prejudice, you understand? I'll strip you of your pension if I have to go to the Supreme Court.' And he would too."

I was to learn that Queensland's marital affairs had been an in-house FBI joke for years. He had fathered one child each—girls—by three ex-wives and his present wife. He was paying child support on three children and alimony to one ex-wife, in addition to supporting his present menage.

"That old goat Queensland has a more screwed up domestic life than a Hollywood star," one of the other agents told me later. "I don't see how he makes it from payday to payday. It's a mystery to me how he's survived all these years in a straitlaced outfit like this, screwing everything he could overtake and overpower, and getting all those divorces. But the current Mrs. Queensland's not going to let him get rid of her. She told my wife that J.B.'s other wives were wild and ran around and he was able to catch them with other men when he wanted a divorce. But Mildred, number four, says she doesn't run around and she doesn't believe in divorce and he's going to do his duty and stay married and support her and their daughter whether he likes it or not."

Most of the SACs would speak with awe of Queensland's personnel file, a vast catalog of duties he was forbidden to perform: drive a Bureau car, make a Bureau speech, work in a resident agency, sit on a supervisory desk, and other restrictions *ad infinitum*. By the time he had attained twenty years' service, Queensland's file was a rambling history of what an FBI agent should not do, and yet he had survived. It was a sore point with him that he had never been promoted to grade thirteen, the highest pay grade for an investigative agent. Shackled by the restrictions in his personnel file, he had not had the opportunity to screw up anything for several years so he had no recent letters of censure. Several SACs, prior to reading the complete file, had considered submitting his name for promotion and then chickened out after reading it. This confirmed Queensland's opinion that SACs were a gutless lot. Even the most reckless SAC I ever knew, one who was continually on probation and who regularly posted his own letters of censure on the field office bulletin board, backed off from recommending Queensland's promotion after reading the file. "I thought I'd got by with murder in this outfit," the SAC said, "but this guy makes every other fuck-up I ever knew look like a sissy. He threw the furniture out of a hotel room in Chicago during an American Legion parade. He got arrested with two whores in a Bureau car in Cleveland. He's been married four times and the divorces were all stinkers. The wives alleged adultery, brutality, and God knows what else, and he alleged the same thing right back. The last thing he did was shoot his Bureau revolver at a bellboy in Tulsa for selling him a bottle of bootleg booze that Queensland said tasted like horse pee. This guy has led a charmed life in this outfit. He's gotten away with enough stuff to get a dozen agents fired. They may be just using him to try to trap me. (*They* were the SAC's enemies at SOG.) To hell with that raise."

"Well," said Queensland, "I should have known better than to expect help from that cowardly son of a bitch. I decided to hit up the Old Man personally the next time I went In Service."

"Do you go in to see the Director often, Mr. Queensland?" At that time, when I was relatively new in the office, I attempted to be respectful to my elders. Later on I called him "Jugbutt" or "J.B." like everyone else.

"Oh, hell yes. Every time I go In Service. Why, if I didn't go in to see him every time I went to Washington, he'd think I was mad at him, so the last time I went, I decided to hit him up personally about the raise and quit screwing around with these soda jerkers and ribbon clerks he sends out as SACs."

"What happened?"

"Everything went fine at first. I bullshitted him along a little bit, you know, about the old days of the 1930s that he likes to talk about—John Dillinger and Pretty Boy Floyd and that stuff."

"And Melvin Purvis?" That was the name of the SAC who led the Dillinger assassination team. "Do you talk to him about Melvin Purvis?"

"Hell, no. Not about Melvin Purvis. If you go in there, don't ever mention *his* name. That would be like dropping a bomb into Mount Vesuvius. Melvin got his name in the news too much to suit the Director. But that's another story. After I got him in a pretty good mood, I mentioned that I was probably the only agent in the Bureau with twenty years service who wasn't in grade thirteen."

"What did he say about that?"

"Well, he didn't say anything specific. He seldom says anything specific unless it's 'no.' He acted sort of surprised to hear it and sort of interested. He made some notes in ink in my file and I thought I had him by the scrotum sure as hell, till I blew it. I just couldn't keep my goddam mouth shut."

"What did you say, Mr. Queensland?"

"It was one of those stupid things. He was talking about old times when the Bureau was small and how it was so big now and how important it was for all of us to face up to changing times and current responsibilities. Then, instead of keeping my mouth shut and sort of fading out the door, I said something like, 'Yes, Mr. Hoover, I sure wish we could go back to the good old days when you could personally keep track of everything that was going on.' As soon as the words were out of my mouth I knew I'd ripped my drawers. He swelled up like a toad and really let me have it. It was almost as bad as the chewing out he gave me after the Tulsa thing. 'I want you to know, Queensland,' he said, 'I still personally keep track of everything that goes on in this Bureau! I still know personally *everything* that goes on! I still personally *run* this Bureau!' And all the time he's talking, he's scratching out the stuff he's written in ink in my file, and he wrote in some more stuff. When I finally managed to escape, I said to myself, 'Queensland, you've screwed it up again. You'll be in grade twelve till you die. If you stay on duty till you're ninety years old, you'll still be in grade twelve.' "

6

The Importance of Being Ignorant

Like the majority of my contemporaries in the Bureau I soon developed a strong antipathy toward office inspections and inspectors. There were two kinds of field office inspections: Routine ones occurred about once a year, and "special" ones dropped on an office out of the blue anytime a special problem arose. As I describe them in turn, keep in mind that a routine inspection could turn into a bloodbath of the "special" type in a twinkling if an inspector unearthed a particularly stinky infraction of Bureau rules or policy.

I developed the opinion over the years that what the Director looked for in his SACs and ASACs—and he picked them all personally—were obedient miracle men who could perform the following functions without breaking any of his multifarious rules and regulations: (1) handle all the administrative work of running an office—mainly ensuring that the deadlines for all reports and communications were met, (2) personally ramrod field investigations of "major cases" to successful conclusions, (3) control the news media to the extent that every reference to the FBI and its Director was laudatory, and (4) constantly increase the office's "statistical accomplishments." Substantive errors could be easily committed in attempting to perform any of those functions, because "Bureau policy" dictated what a substantive error was, and on many occasions SOG laid down the policy *ex post facto*, after a SAC or ASAC had already made some irrevocable move. Some bleeding-heart, sob-sister SACs and ASACs referred to this practice as "second guessing" —generally after they had made a wrong decision and were made to suffer for it.

A SAC was technically in command of a field office, but in actuality he had no real independence unless he chose to break the Bureau rules. He was the Director's "personal representative"; therefore he was rarely allowed to have original thoughts. He was continually haunted by the fear of being second-guessed by some official at SOG, generally the Director. A field investigation could start out well with the full approval of SOG and then go sour because bad publicity appeared in the news media or a person of influence made a complaint. Then, in its infinite wisdom, SOG would decree that the whole thing had been mishandled from the beginning and the SAC must pay with his head or, to use a more common, earthy expression, "his ass." Then the Stukas would be over his office, a wave of paratroopers in the guise of goons would drop from the skies, and a "special" inspection would begin.

The most important criteria used in judging a field office during a routine inspection were the statistical accomplishments: the monetary value of fines, savings, and recoveries, and the number of convictions and apprehended fugitives, to name the most important. The "stats" had to be higher every year, or the office was in trouble. Stats had no memory. Once used, they were discarded. Yesterday's accomplishments were soon forgotten. Statistical history became ancient history very quickly. The Director once said to a SAC, "I don't care what you did for me last year, last month, or last week. I want to know, what have you done for me today?" This attitude caused some SACs and ASACs to do all sorts of weird things to increase statistical accomplishments, bringing the formula I = R back into play.

The senior inspector, prior to his departure from SOG to lead a squad on an office inspection, always got in touch with the Director, Mr. Tolson, and all the assistant directors to inquire if any of them thought the field office had any particular problems that should be delved into. If any of those individuals expressed derogatory opinions about the SAC or the ASAC—such as the observation that one of them seemed "complacent" or "weak"—then the head goon knew that there was a contract out for that individual, and he had better find enough substantive errors on the individual to justify his removal, dismissal, or demotion. If the inspector failed to execute the contract, he risked his own future, because a contract would very likely be issued for him.

Some inspectors came in quiet as mice, masking any predatory intentions with smiles and handshakes. They would accept cut-rate hotel accommodations and free booze and free meals and the use of a new automobile borrowed from a dealer. If there were no contracts out, they might tell the SAC confidentially how many subs they had to find, and the SAC would then try to arrange for them to be found in cases supervised on desks other than his own. Often, after the inspector had found his quota of subs, he would disappear quietly back to SOG and write up a report mildly critical of some unimportant phase of the field office operations to create the illusion he had really given the office a thorough going over. He had to find *something*. After all, he was an inspector, and no office was perfect. The SAC would get a gentle letter of remonstrance, and that would be the end of it for another year, unless something unexpected cropped up. The inspector would have created his illusion, and no one in the office would be really hurt, except the supervisors and agents whose subs had been written up in the quota. They possibly had the feeling they had gotten the shaft, especially if they were due for raises in the near future. Letters of censure of any kind generally delayed grade raises for at least ninety days. But *somebody* had to get the shaft, didn't he?

Sometimes, however, the inspectors were slyer than they acted. They would depart with a full quota of unimportant subs, leaving the office with a false sense of security. When they got back to SOG they would write a report lambasting everyone from the SAC down to the lowest clerk, and then the excrement would hit the fan and splatter the office in an unexpected deluge.

The special inspections—as opposed to the routine—were generally caused by some alleged violation or problem being brought to the attention of SOG by a complaint from a citizen, a story in the news media, or, very frequently, an anonymous letter from an employee. In the case of anonymous letters the inspector always seemed much more interested in identifying the writer than investigating the allegation set forth in the letter, because generally the allegation was made against the SAC or ASAC, individuals personally appointed by the Director. It was much safer to identify and discredit the letter writer than to let some lowly Field hand imply disrespectfully and anonymously that the Director had been wrong in making an appointment. Flaws in SACs and ASACs were supposed to be found by the Director or one of his personal representatives, not by disgruntled employees. SOG generally sent out a hard-nosed, mad-dog type of inspector on these specials, one who would burst into the office like the North Korean assassin who charged the heroic Major Frank Sinatra from the bathroom in the movie *The Manchurian Candidate*, chopping wildly in a frenzied karate attack.

Not long after being sent to my second office, I underwent an inspection of the "special" variety. This was precipitated by an anonymous letter alleging that the SAC and the ASAC were incompetent and had falsified some office records in the course of an investigation to apprehend a badly wanted fugitive.

The SAC was the tall, handsome man who had warned me on my arrival against "laying any pipe" in his office. I always thought of him as the Hawk because of his tendency to pounce on anything that looked like an infraction of rules on the part of Bureau employees other than himself. I have previously alluded to his mutilated English, which did not deter him from making public speeches. I was present when he said to a church group, "I was expecting Reverend Higginbottom to help me with this here program but he apparently hasn't came yet. I should have knew I could not depend on a preacher for anything, especially a Baptist preacher." His audience was Baptist, and there were several ministers present.

Prior to his elevation to SAC he had been a firearms instructor and a member of the palace guard in one of the large field offices. During his interview with the Director prior to promotion, he must have kept his mouth shut and let the Old Man do all the talking. His shortcomings as an administrator soon became apparent to everyone in the office. His theory of the SAC role was primitive, to say the least. He concentrated mainly on assigning stenographers to agents who wanted to dictate and to inspecting Bureau cars for mechanical defects. In most field offices a senior stenographer assigned stenographers and a clerk handled the car maintenance. But the Hawk understood these two simple tasks and concentrated on them.

His assistant, the ASAC, generally known as the Sparrow, was a different bag of tricks altogether. Small of build and cunning, he had been badly frightened once in the Bureau and sent to a doghouse office. I asked someone who had known him what had been the cause of his trouble. "It was over an expense voucher. They caught him with his claw in the tambourine," the source said obscurely. The Sparrow had been rehabilitated in his doghouse office, however, and was now building nests higher and higher in the Bureau tree.

The impressive-looking but dumb SAC and the less impressive-looking but cunning ASAC arrived in the office at the same time, a masterpiece of administrative mismatching if there ever was one.

After I joined the office, the SAC received a telephone call from another field office telling him where a badly wanted fugitive was supposed to be staying in a nearby motel. The SAC dawdled around several hours before sending agents to check out the information. The fugitive, whose name was Dobransky, had checked out and disappeared an hour before the agents arrived. He was not to be apprehended until several months later, elsewhere. It dawned on the SAC that he had committed a booboo. He prevailed upon some of the agents to change the times on office records—the agents' "Number 3" cards—to conceal the fact that he had delayed sending the group to the motel. He was not the most popular SAC in the Bureau, so someone in the office wrote an anonymous letter to the Director blabbing about his falsification of records and other shortcomings. The goons dropped in almost immediately. The senior inspector decided to interview every agent who had participated in the fugitive operation in any way. I happened to fall into that unhappy group, having participated in a surveillance of the motel the night after the fugitive disappeared.

While we were sitting around in the big agents' room waiting for the inspector's one-at-a-time summons, Harris, who had ambitions to rise in the Bureau, wrung his hands and said, "I don't know what to tell him."

"Don't tell him anything," one of the older agents advised him. "There's an old adage which says, 'There are no deaf and dumb people in the penitentiary.' A lot of the people who get into trouble during inspections are those who have heard a little something about whatever the inspection's about and then can't resist talking about it. Tell him you don't know anything at all."

"He'll think I'm crazy. He knows I know something."

"He doesn't know what you know. And all you know is about changing those cards, stuff derogatory to the SAC. He doesn't want to hear that. What he wants to find out is who wrote the anonymous letter, so he can bust his ass."

"I've got to tell him something."

"Tell him you don't know anything."

"He'll think I'm dumb."

"That's exactly what you want him to think. Tell him you don't know what's going on in the office. Tell him you just come in every morning and pick up the stuff from your work box and leave. You come back to the office late. You don't talk to anybody. You don't know what's going on."

"I don't want him to think I'm dumb. I'm trying to go up in this outfit. I've got to tell him something."

"You'll be sorry."

Harris was called next, and we waited for what seemed

a long time for him to reappear. We wandered around the big room filled with agents' desks and occasionally got a drink from the water cooler. Those who were smokers smoked. Some stood at the windows looking down at the street below, where the free people of the outside world went about their everyday affairs just as though nothing were going on. Harris finally came out of the front office, flushed and upset. "He wants you next," he said to me. "I've got to write a memo."

"You see?" said the older agent. "And after you write that memo, you'll write another memo explaining what you meant in the first memo and so on and so on." He turned to me. "Now, get smart. Be dumb."

The inspector had appropriated the SAC's office. There was a broad desk, a leather couch against the wall, an American flag drooping at one end of the desk, and a large color photograph of the Director on the wall behind the desk. In front of the desk was a single straight chair.

"Sit down," the inspector said.

I sat in the straight chair and looked at the inspector. He was a handsome man, well dressed in a dark suit and white shirt, with black hair turning a becoming gray at the temples.

He smiled at me disarmingly and said, "I need some help from you in this investigation."

I had not been an agent very long at the time and had never experienced an office inspection, but luckily I had spent several months as a clerk at SOG. It had been pounded into my head by the older clerks that the only way you could "help" an inspector was to hurt yourself or somebody else. I did not say anything.

When I did not volunteer any remarks, he asked me some general questions about my background, how long I had been in the office, and so forth. All that information was in my personnel file which was on the desk in front of him. Suddenly he said to me sharply, "Did you hear that this office missed a badly wanted fugitive named Dobransky recently because of negligence on the part of the Special Agent in Charge?"

"No, sir."

"Don't tell me you didn't hear anything about the Dobransky case."

"Yes, sir, I mean, no, sir."

The inspector frowned at me. "What do you mean? Did you hear anything about the case or not? Yes or no."

"Yes."

"O.K. Did you hear that the office missed him?"

"No."

"You didn't?" The inspector expressed surprise. "Then what did you hear about the case?"

"I heard we almost caught him."

The inspector frowned again. "Are you trying to get funny with me?"

"What do you mean, sir?"

"Goddam it, don't answer a question with a question! I know that you participated in the case to the extent that you and an agent named Porter sat in a parked car all night on surveillance at that motel after the fugitive had fled. Is that right?"

"Yes."

"Let's see." He looked down at some notes. "Porter told me that during the time you were on that surveillance you and he discussed how the Special Agent in Charge had screwed up the case by not getting men out there soon enough. Is that so?"

"No."

"Then somebody is lying, right?"

"Yes," I said.

He pounced. "Who is it, then? You or Porter? Which one of you is lying?"

"Neither one," I said.

The inspector turned beet red. The inference was clear that I was calling him a liar. "Are you disputing my word?" He slapped his hand down on the notepad in front of him.

"Porter is out there in the big agents' room," I said. "We can call him in here and straighten out what he said."

"I'm running this goddamned interview, not 'we,' " the inspector said. "Do you think the Special Agent in Charge of this office is incompetent?"

"No."

"Did you ever tell anyone he was incompetent?"

"No."

'Did you ever hear anyone in this office say he was incompetent?"

"No."

"Dammit, there's been all sorts of talk in this office among the agents, clerks, and everyone else that the Special Agent in Charge is incompetent and you know it. Don't tell me you've never heard it."

"I'm sorry, but I never heard it."

"What do you mean, *you're sorry* you never heard it?"

"I don't really mean that I regret not having heard it, but from the way you phrased your question by starting off with 'Don't tell me—' "

"Dammit, don't tell me how to phrase my questions. You must be pretty goddam dumb, you know that?"

"Yes, sir."

"Now about the anonymous letter . . ."

"I don't know anything about any anonymous letter,"

I said. "I never heard anybody say anything about an anonymous letter and I never wrote one myself. I don't know anything about any anonymous letter. Period."

The inspector looked at me for a long time. "You know, Schott, I bet you're the type of guy who gets to the office very early mornings and picks up your stuff out of your work box and leaves. Then you come back late and go home. I bet you never talk to anybody about anything or hear anybody say anything about anything, is that right?"

"Yes, sir," I said.

"You know, that's just the type of guy your friend Porter says he is. Isn't that goddam remarkable?"

"If you say so, sir."

This time the inspector got so mad he almost snarled. "You're not fooling me a goddam bit with that dumb act. Get out of here and tell that guy who's writing the memo to get his butt in here with it." As an afterthought, he said, "And don't you go anywhere either. I may have something else to say to you and your friend."

I went back to the big agents' room. Harris was standing there with a memo in his hand he had hastily typed. "He wants to see you and your memo," I said to Harris. Harris hurried toward the SAC's office. He came back in a few minutes carrying a crumpled ball of paper in his hand. "He wadded up the memo after he read it and threw it at me. I've got to type it over. He wants to see Queensland next." Harris hurried on to the back of the room, where the typewriters were.

"Well, it's about time he talked to somebody who can give him some real information," Queensland said as he waddled toward the door.

Half an hour later Queensland emerged from the interview, snorting irritably. "He wants to see you and your goddam memo again," he said to Harris.

Harris ran back down the hall with the new memo he had been typing on furiously.

The inspector had riled Queensland, that was plain. "That goddam ribbon clerk! He looks like something the Director got as a prize in a box of Cracker Jacks," he said. " 'Mr. Queensland,' " Jugbutt mimicked the inspector, " 'I have some very reliable information that you wrote an anonymous letter to the Director in which you referred to the Special Agent in Charge of this office as a dumb son of a bitch. Is that true?' 'No, Mr. Inspector,' I said, 'that is not true.' 'Well, then,' he says, 'have you ever in conversation referred to him as a dumb son of a bitch?' 'Yes, I have,' I said, 'on numerous occasions.' He got all excited and picked up his pencil and asked, 'Who did you say this to?' I said, 'On several occasions I have told the Special Agent in Charge to his face that I thought he was a dumb son of a bitch. Also, I have told the Assistant Special Agent in Charge and the supervisor that they were dumb sons of bitches to their faces. I don't write anybody any goddam anonymous letters.' That brought on a rather lively exchange, I must say. An exchange that culminated in my observation that I didn't think the inspector was the smartest son of a bitch I had ever run into in this vale of tears, either, and that I intended to write a memo to the Director on him immediately and tell the Director about him personally the next time I was in Washington." Queensland picked up the telephone and ordered a stenographer directly from the steno pool. "No, honey," he said to someone at the other end of the line, "I'm not going to clear it with the SAC. You just get your own pretty little tokus out here with a pencil and notebook."

In a few minutes the chief stenographer herself appeared, notebook in hand. "O.K., Jug," she said. "Keep it short. I don't have all day."

Then Jugbutt Queensland dictated a memorandum to the "personal attention of the Director," and it was one of his finest performances. As we watched and listened, he walked around his desk, waving his arms, describing to the Director in detail who in the office, including the inspector, the SAC, the ASAC, and the supervisor, he had called sons of bitches and why, giving exhaustive rationale for having done so in each instance.

After he finished the stenographer closed her book and said, "Thank you, Mr. Queensland. That was the very best dictation I've ever had. You can call me anytime you're in town, but leave that son of a bitch of an inspector at home."

Queensland collapsed in a paroxysm of laughter. He laughed so hard he swallowed a piece of his cigar and almost choked, his face turning blue. We beat him on the back while he snorted and huffed like a walrus and finally got his breath back.

Just then, Harris reappeared from the hall. He again had a wadded up ball of paper in his hand. "He wants Davis next," he said and again headed back toward the typewriters.

That went on all day. Harris would go in with a memo, reappear in a few minutes, call out the next man's name, and then go back to the typewriter. Shortly after 6 P.M. he emerged for the last time, without the memo. "He finally accepted it," Harris said. "He said the rest of you guys could go home."

I followed Harris into the elevator as we left the building.

"What did you say in the memo he finally accepted?" I asked.

"Well, it finally became clear to me that I really didn't know anything about the boss being incompetent or anything, so that's what I said. I think it was kind of a matter of semantics that got me crossways with him at first. When I handed that last memo, after my thoughts had become clarified on the matter, he was very cordial. He said he was going to note in my file that I had been extremely cooperative in the course of his investigation."

As a result of that inspection, nothing very much happened. The writer of the anonymous letter was never identified. A few weeks later the Hawk was transferred to another office as SAC to continue his assignment of stenographers and inspection of cars in a different setting. I saw him several years later at a police meeting when he was running another office. He wrinkled his handsome brow and asked, "Ain't you the one who married the airlines stewardess?"

"No, I married the newspaper reporter."

His brow cleared. "I should've knew it would be somebody strange," he said.

The Sparrow stayed around as ASAC for another year or so and then was promoted to SAC of another office. He may be out there somewhere now building a nest higher in the tree, trying to get his claw into a tambourine.

7

"I'm Not Too Heavy, I'm Too Short"

"In making the agents take off weight, he has saved many of their lives."

—CLYDE A. TOLSON,
Associate Director, FBI

The Director's campaign against the fat boys in the FBI began, to the best of my recollection, in the late 1950s. The campaign, which developed into a guerrilla war, was still being waged when I retired in late 1971.

I don't know the true genesis of Mr. Hoover's preoccupation with weight as a personnel problem. The "authorized version," which came down from Crime Records or some other dream factory at SOG, was that Mr. Hoover himself became overweight and after losing some excess poundage under doctor's orders felt so much better than he decided to share the benefits of weight reduction with the special agents, whether they liked it or not. That is the *authorized* version, as I have said. There is another story of how he conceived the weight reduction idea that makes more sense to me as the true version because it illustrates the sensitivity, or susceptibility, to trivial remarks that seemed so characteristic of him.

The story is that a lady visitor from Canada, observing a public firearms demonstration at the FBI Academy, noted that one of the firearms instructors looked wide in the rear and fat in the gut. She wrote a bread and butter letter to the Director thanking him for the Academy tour, et cetera, et cetera, and in closing put a tiny drop of poison in the sandwich. "However, I must say, your FBI agents are not as slim and trim as our Mounties. I saw several of your men on the firing range at Quantico who seemed to be heavier than they should be."

That letter, allegedly, launched the Director's campaign against the potguts and fatasses in the Bureau. The campaign was known in the Bureau as the "weight program." Just after the program began, an agent of my acquaintance came up two pounds overweight on his annual physical examination. He smiled. Who would make a fuss over a mere two pounds? He should have known who would. Those two pounds cost him approximately a thousand dollars each. The Director delayed a grade raise to which the agent was entitled for over a year until after his *next* regular physical examination. After receiving that slap on the wrist, that particular agent made sure he was "within the desirable weight range" on every physical exam forever after.

The enforcement of any new Bureau rule, especially in its initial stages, habitually took the form of a bloody pogrom against all who were caught violating the rule even slightly—the old "hang the pickpocket" approach. Then, habitually, as time went by and newer rules were hatched in the Director's brain, the pressure would ease on older rules and be transferred to newer ones. The weight program, however, remained a hanging matter from the very beginning until the Director died, more than a dozen years later. The standard to be met was a schedule published by the Metropolitan Life Insurance Company, which gave a desirable weight range for males, taking into consideration their height and frame size—small, medium, or large. At least half the mature male population of the United States must be overweight, according to this schedule.

I have always been on the slim side; nevertheless, I had to lose weight before every physical examination to stay within the desirable limits for my height. I had the misfortune of being five feet eleven *and a half* inches tall. If the Bureau had given me the benefit of the extra half-inch and called me six feet, I would have been within the desirable at 175 pounds. But the Administrative Division was not giving away any half-inches. They had to "improve" on the schedule. I had to meet the weight standard for five feet eleven inches, period. That meant I was slightly overweight at 175 pounds. This may seem like a picayune, insignificant technicality to soft-headed civilians outside the Bureau, but arguing about the two or three pounds involved in that half inch could have caused me trouble. It was wiser to dine on cereal with skim milk for a week or so before a physical, lose a few pounds, and get into the five feet eleven weight range than to engage in a righteous paper battle with the Bureau that could end in a transfer to Butte.

Of course, the trolls on the heights of SOG, vying for the favor of the Director, tried to outdo each other in losing weight. I visited there for two weeks' In Service training during the first year of the weight program and noticed that many of them looked like concentration camp inmates, their skinny necks sticking up from loose shirt collars and their suits hanging loosely on emaciated frames. Former athletes, especially football players, had the worst of it. I talked with a former Notre Dame lineman in the hall of the Justice Building—there were a lot of Notre Dame graduates in the Bureau after that institution awarded the Director an honorary degree in 1942—and he said woefully, "At my height, according to the weight schedule, I'm not supposed to weigh over 185 pounds, even in the big frame. Hell, I weigh 185 pounds from my waist down."

I noticed, however, that there were still a few plump supervisors left at SOG. They all seemed to slink down the halls hugging the wall, ready to jump into an open doorway if they saw an inspector approaching.

The weight program became the *raison d'être* for more chicanery and deception than ever before in the Field. Because the weight program became such a vital issue— affecting promotions, transfers, and pay raises—strategies had to be devised to neutralize it. Some handled the matter on paper by extending their heights several inches, enlarging their frames from medium to large, or just lying about their weights. These ruses could be carried out in the Field with the collusion of examining doctors and members of office supervisory staffs. Some SACs exiled hopelessly fat agents to distant resident agencies and tried to forget about them. One of the major misfortunes that could happen to a field office was the arrival of a naturally thin SAC who was dedicated to the enforcement of weight rules. Rotund agents would go on crash diets and try to hide. They would shrink down behind their desks, blowing out their breath, trying to appear smaller whenever the SAC would charge through the agents' bullpen area. In the large offices—New York, Los Angeles, Chicago—fantastic feats of avoidance and invisibility could be managed successfully. But in small offices—Mobile, El Paso, Butte—complete avoidance was impossible. In the small offices fat agents prayed for a fat SAC who would understand their problems and be so busy trying to create his own illusion of skinniness by extending his height, enlarging his frame, or suborning the medical examiner and his staff that he would leave them alone.

One of the great weight illusionists of the Bureau was Charles Elfinbein of the Washington Field Office. I should explain that the Washington Field Office, generally called WFO, is the field office that handles investigations within the District of Columbia. WFO is functionally part of the Field but is geographically too close to Bureau headquarters for its own good. In the old regime it caught more than its share of the radioactive fallout from the volcano of knowledge next door.

WFO was housed in the Old Post Office Building (OPO) at Twelfth Street and Pennsylvania Avenue, Northwest, an architectural antique of blackened gray stone as dank and gloomy as Macbeth's castle. OPO was a vast, high-ceilinged building that the Bureau had converted into a beehive of cubbyhole offices and "pool" areas by building partitions and lowering ceilings with plywood. In summer some rooms were cooled with window air conditioners. Movable rotary floor fans encased in protective screens were scattered about to keep the sticky air moving. The constant whirr of electric motors filled the place. In winter electric heaters replaced the fans. Then the employees scorched their shins up close and froze their tails at a distance. WFO was a damp, sultry place in summer and a damp chilly place in winter.

Elfinbein was one of the old-timers of the WFO, a cliff dweller, born and raised in Washington. Practically all of the agents who listed WFO as their office of preference were cliff dwellers or married to cliff dwellers. No one else ever volunteered to work there. Elfinbein, better known as Elfie to his friends, was a florid, overweight man who did not suffer from the chills of winter but made up for it in summer. When the weather became warm, Elfie broke out in prickly heat on tender, intimate areas of his body and smelled like a skunk in a Turkish bath. Occasionally he would lose control and scratch his crotch or armpits vigorously, moaning and grunting with relief. This uninhibited conduct brought shocked, embarrassed looks from the stenographers and sniggers from the agents. His musky odor offended everyone, especially the girls. Some of them complained about his conduct and smell to the chief stenographer, who spoke to Elfie's supervisor about it. The supervisor called Elfie in and gave it to him straight, prescribing massive applications of deodorant and Desenex.

"You've just got to cure that jock itch, Elfie," he said. "I may be able to protect you to a certain extent on the armpit scratching and even on the BO, but there just ain't no way to justify that ball-scratching. It verges on obscenity. That ball-scratching's got to go."

Elfie stomped out of the supervisor's office, kicked one of the floor fans across the room, and shoved it under his desk so that when he sat at the desk he straddled the churning fan. Some of the other agents in the room, deprived of the fan's cooling effects, stood in front of Elfie's desk and cursed and reviled him, but he sat there and stubbornly refused to release it.

Several of the agents complained to the supervisor, who gave them scant encouragement. "I'll try to requisition another fan. I'm going to keep his crotch cool if everybody else out there melts. If one of those stenos complains about that ball-scratching over there across the street, the goons will run in here with their machetes slashing at everything that moves."

So Elfie kept his private fan and became known as "Cool Crotch" Elfinbein. Although the arrangement added to the general discomfort, it did reduce the stink and minimize the scratching and animal-like grunting that had previously marred Elfie's behavior.

When the weight program crashed in like one of those mysterious rockets in *1984*, Elfie was still almost a year away from his retirement age and at least thirty pounds overweight. To add to his problems, the Director decided just then to appoint a new SAC to WFO, a dedicated martinet, about as tall as a cavalry saber and just as thin, a man with no heart for the overburdened. The new SAC immediately installed clinical scales in his office and personally measured and weighed all his agents. The agents had a choice. They could strip and be weighed naked or remain modestly clothed and be given credit for a three-pound deduction for the weight of their clothes.

"The son of a bitch mashes that measuring rod down on your head to shorten your height and then tries to stand on the scales with you to read the weight. He hates anybody over five feet seven inches tall," a tall, fat agent complained.

When Elfie waddled in, sweating and grunting, he immediately began removing his clothes. The SAC, repelled by the prospect of looking at Elfie naked, generously offered him a five-pound clothing reduction.

"Well, my clothes are all wet with sweat, you see," Elfie said. "Water makes them heavier. I think I ought to have at least eight pounds credit."

"Oh, all right," said the SAC, "but don't tell the rest of them." He knew that Elfie could not have made the weight with a twenty-pound reduction. He was right. Elfinbein was twenty-two pounds overweight.

"It's not that I'm really overweight," said Elfie. "It's just that I'm too goddam short. If I were five inches taller with this same weight, I would be right in the desirable."

"Tell you what," said the SAC, displaying that sadistic sense of humor he was famous for, "if you can grow five inches in thirty days, it's O.K. with me. I'm giving you thirty days to get into the desirable range and I'm setting up a tickler to weigh you again then. If you haven't made the desirable weight in thirty days, I'm referring this matter across the street to the Administrative Division."

Elfie knew that meant disaster. He had hidden from the draft in the FBI during World War II and therefore lacked the veteran's right to appeal to Civil Service. He served "at the pleasure of the Director," and he could foresee that the Director's displeasure would be intense if he did not lose the weight. His career would be snipped off just short of retirement.

For several days Elfie tried desperately to diet. He breakfasted on sugarless coffee and dry toast, then burped disconsolately until noon, when he would have a bowl of thin soup. For dinner he ate a thin ham sandwich and drank a glass of skimmed milk. Then he would roll and toss all night dreaming about food. He even quit drinking beer. One day, after more than a week of this regimen, he lost control suddenly while walking past a restaurant that had in the window a huge round of beef rotating over a grill. The beef was crusty and dark brown on the outside and red and juicy in the middle. Elfie ran into the restaurant and gobbled up two large sandwiches and gulped two schooners of beer. "Screw the weight program," he said to himself and ordered a slab of apple pie topped with hot cheese.

As he walked back to the office, his craving for food satisfied for the first time in over a week, a voice kept saying to him, "Elfie, you're not going to make it this way. You got to go around that nutty SAC. You've got to use your brain instead of your body, because your body has gone out of control."

Wandering along Ninth Street, a thoroughfare lined with burlesque houses, hot dog joints, and pawnshops, he stopped in front of a secondhand clothing store. Deep in his brain an idea churned slowly and suddenly broke through the surface to burst like a star shell over no-man's-land. He entered the store.

"What's the biggest dark suit you got?" he asked the proprietor.

"I got lots of big suits, my friend. I can fit you. You're a big guy, but it won't take the biggest."

"Now look," said Elfie, "I don't want a suit that fits me. I want one that's too big for me, see? And it's got to be a dark conservative suit. I normally wear a size forty-eight jacket so we got to go bigger than that."

The proprietor shrugged. The customer was going to a costume party or had a comic part in a play. He searched the racks and finally found a suit that satisfied Elfie. It was dark gray with a good brand label; the jacket was size fifty-two. When buttoned, the jacket hung down in front in a slack fold and the pants were at least three inches too big in the waist. Taking off the jacket, Elfie backed up to the mirror and twisted his neck to study his rear end. "It's got more folds and wrinkles than an old elephant's ass," he said.

"We can fix it, my friend," said the proprietor. "A little taken out here and there . . ."

"No," said Elfie. "Don't alter anything but the sleeves and trouser lengths. They've got to be right. Leave the rest of the suit as is. And I'll need a great big white shirt too, so when I button it there will be a lot of slack around my neck."

Working through his rabbi at SOG, Elfie wangled an appointment with the Director without going through his SAC. When he appeared at the Director's office lugging a notebook, he was wearing his oversize clothing. They let him in without question. There were a lot of people around the halls those days who seemed to have shrunk in their clothes, but this was the worst they had seen.

"I just wanted to come by and tell you how much I appreciate your instituting this weight program," Elfie said to the Director. "I've lost twenty-five pounds and feel twenty-five years younger. My doctor says I need to lose another twenty pounds but I ought to spread it over the next six or eight months. My wife went on a diet the same time I did and she's lost fifteen pounds. Just this morning she said to me, 'Thank God for Mr. Hoover. He saved my life. Tell him I'm praying for him.'"

The Director scribbled blue ink vigorously in Elfie's file and shook hands with him warmly when they parted a few minutes later.

At the end of the prescribed thirty days, the SAC at WFO weighed Elfie again and found he had lost only a few pounds. He fired off a memorandum to the Administrative Division saying that Special Agent Elfinbein was not complying with the weight program and suggested that severe administrative action be taken against him.

The next day the SAC received a guarded telephone call from a friend in the Administrative Division. "You may want to tear up this memo on your fat boy," the friend said.

"Why?"

"There's some fresh blue ink in this guy's personnel

file. He talked to The Man recently and the ink says not to make an issue of his weight until his next routine physical check-up which is almost a year off."

The SAC knew what he had to do. "Send me back the memo in a plain envelope marked 'personal,'" he said. "I'll tear it up as well as the copy in my file."

"I thought you might want to do that," his friend said.

Downstairs Elfie was seated at his desk, the fan whirring between his knees. His crotch was comfortably cool and his stomach was pleasantly full. He had had spaghetti and meatballs for lunch and two schooners of beer. He was sleepy, but the roar of the fan would keep him awake.

═══► 8

The Necessary Evils

"Resident agents are necessary evils. . . . One who is not dedicated has the greatest sinecure in the world."
—an observation allegedly made by J. EDGAR HOOVER at some time or other during his long reign as Director, according to Bureau legend

"A resident agent," a field supervisor once told me with great seriousness, "is a goddam parasite. He is the most overpaid individual in the world. After he is sent out to a resident agency, you never see him again except a couple of times a year—at the annual agents' conference and the office Christmas party. Occasionally you hear his voice on the telephone telling you lies. You send him out to cover an important lead with a Bureau deadline on it and he disappears. You call and call. The phone in his office doesn't answer. The dispatcher at his favorite police department, where he and the chief are golfing buddies, hasn't seen him in a week. It's a goddam lie. At that very moment, he and the chief are out in a golf cart at the country club, drinking beer and swatting the little white ball. But the dispatcher won't squeal on him. You call his home. His wife *never* knows where he is. An RA wife learns to lie as well as her husband before long. Finally he calls you, in the middle of the night. The son of a bitch wakes you up at home in the middle of the night, just before the deadline, to tell you a long, sad, involved, heart-breaking tale of woe about why he can't make the deadline—a witness is missing, somebody has left the country without a trace, records have been burned up in a courthouse fire—I've heard all those excuses and more.

"While he's talking, you can hear music and drunk women laughing in the background. The son of a bitch is out in a honky-tonk somewhere, living it up. 'Where are you?' you ask, 'there seems to be a lot of noise in the background.'

" 'It's the only place in Pittsburg open at this time of night.'

" 'Pittsburg? Where in the hell is Pittsburg? You haven't wandered all the way up to Pennsylvania to screw off, have you?'

" 'Pittsburg is between Daingerfield and Mount Vernon,' he says. 'Everybody knows that. I'm in an all night café.'

"You think to yourself, 'It's a café, all right, but the only food they serve there is the peanuts to go with the beer or those hot Polish sausages that give you indigestion. 'Get the goddam lead covered!' you scream at him and roll and toss the rest of the night while he drinks beer in that honky-tonk.

"A resident agent is a pain in the ass. He doesn't sew, weave, or spin. He just screws around and lets his cases get delinquent. If he covers big towns on his road trip, he has merchants conned to give him discounts on watches, clothes, and appliances. He can rent the best room in any hotel or motel in his territory for five bucks a night. He buys all kinds of stuff in country markets, loading his Bureau car down with eggs, cantaloupes, and country hams. All RAs are con men. If they're not con men when you send them out, they turn into con men. If I were Director, I would close every resident agency in the Bureau."

"They are necessary evils," I said. "The Director has proclaimed them so. They simply must be dedicated."

"They are dedicated to screwing off," he said.

Agents assigned to one-man RAs—working out of their homes in hamlets in western Oklahoma and Kansas and the Far West, getting into the headquarters city only once or twice a year—tended to wander off the FBI screen after a while and go native. They would appear in headquarters city dressed like cowboys or sheepherders or reservation Indians wearing plaid shirts and cowboy boots and large hunks of silver and turquoise jewelry. Many SACs encouraged these characters to stay home and visit headquarters as infrequently as possible.

"I don't care if he's driving his Bureau car as a taxi or hauling hay in it out there on the reservation," a SAC said to me about one of the exotic RAs. "I just want him to stay out of sight. He knows everybody in his territory and gets his work done, but he looks and acts more like a Texas Ranger or Indian scout than an FBI agent."

Sometimes those assigned to two-man RAs deteriorated more than the loners. After an extended period of time together they began hating each other's guts. In one instance the two came to a logical solution. One worked days and the other worked nights, and they left notes for each other about telephone calls and messages. They would go for weeks without having to look at each other.

There was a two-man RA in which the pair became so antagonistic they built a plywood partition dividing their single office. Each occupied a separate cubicle. Just above their desks was a square opening in the wall with a flat board shelf across the bottom. On this shelf they placed the telephone. When they were in their cubicles at the same time they took turns answering the phone. The phone would ring and a disembodied voice would say, "It's your turn." A hand from the other side would reach up and take the receiver. The answerer might say, "It's for you." The receiver would then pass between upraised hands. In this way they could communicate without having to look at each other. One of them still retained the vestiges of a sense of humor after several years of this. I once asked him how it started.

"You remember that old movie *The Gold Rush* where the two guys were playing poker in a cabin during a blizzard and they were so hungry one of them began to look like a big chicken to the other?"

"Yeah."

"Well, one day I was thinking about that in the office and I said, 'Frank, you know what you remind me of? A chicken, that's what. A big funny-looking chicken.' And he says to me, 'Sid, you remind me of a duck. You walk like a duck. You talk like a duck. By God, you must be a duck.' Next day we had the wall built. We even paid for it ourselves."

I spent more than twenty years assigned to the same resident agency—a large one with a dozen or more agents —and although we had some squabbles occasionally no one became more than normally upset at anyone else. Some of the headquarters city supervisors seemed to resent our equanimity. One ASAC referred to us disparagingly as "the Fort Worth Club," but we managed to get along with that creep without sacrificing our good humor, savoir-faire, or aura of Old World charm and dignity.

Several of us, including me, had road-trip territories that caused us to range out into the hinterland frequently and make contact with the rural lawmen—sheriffs, constables, and city marshals of isolated settlements off the main highways. Many of these men have remained my friends over the years.

The Sheriff at Sparta, a small county seat buried in the piney woods of East Texas, was one of my favorite lawmen. He was built like a cypress stump, durable and extremely hard to knock over. His moon-shaped countenance, projecting as it did the gullible, trusting expression of an earnest bumpkin, was deceptive. His voice was in the high range and tended to go higher when he was excited. He had the distinction of having bred and trained the most celebrated pack of bloodhounds in East Texas.

The first time I saw the Sparta Sheriff he was accompanied by Daddy Frank, his man-of-all-work around the jail, a huge black man whose appearance was enough to scare you half to death. Daddy Frank was six feet five inches tall and gaunt of build, with a large shaven head like a black bowling ball. He had one good eye. The other was a blank white bulb in his black face.

I introduced myself to the Sheriff and showed him my FBI credentials.

He held the credentials at arm's length and studied the picture for a long time. "No, I ain't ever seen him around here," he said.

"That's me," I said with embarrassment.

The Sheriff laughed and handed me back the credentials. "Just a joke, little partner. What kind of hep you need?"

I found that the Sheriff was a sociable soul, always

ready to hep another lawman in his work. Over the years he hepped me a lot. Along about six in the evening, after we had done something big, such as arresting a military deserter in the swamp or recovering a stolen car, we would adjourn to his office in the courthouse basement for refreshments. He would get three bottles of Coca Cola from the machine in the hall and carry them back to his office, whistling tunelessly through his teeth. He handed one bottle to me and one to Daddy Frank. Daddy Frank, I had learned, was an ex-convict who had served twenty years on a Texas prison farm for murdering another man and had a mean reputation. He was out of the pen on parole to the Sheriff. Several people had met disaster trying to crawl on the Sheriff's back when Daddy Frank was around. "When you pick and chop cotton for twenty years on a prison farm, you either die or you get real strong," the Sheriff told me once. "Daddy Frank got real strong. I wish I had a nickel for every bale of cotton Daddy Frank made for the State of Texas."

Daddy Frank would take his Coke and go sit on the floor in the corner. The Sheriff would pour about half of his bottle of Coke into a plastic bowl. This he would push under the slobbery nose of his favorite bloodhound, a spayed bitch named Big Mama. Big Mama would lap up the Coke appreciatively, slopping a lot of it on the floor. After drinking the Coke she would stretch out on the floor again, sneeze and burp loudly, and occasionally break wind. When she did, the Sheriff would say, "Dammit, Big Mama, quit talking about the Supreme Court thataway." The Sheriff would then take a bottle of the bourbon he had confiscated from a bootlegger, fill up his bottle and mine with whisky and pour some into a fruit jar for Daddy Frank. We drank the fortified Cokes and watched the shadows of the tall pines lengthen across the courthouse lawn until the greenish iron statue there, a

Confederate cavalry officer on his horse, had faded to a lighter blob in the gathering dark. Then we would go to the jail kitchen and eat the dinner that Mrs. Sheriff cooked for her family and the prisoners. She would sniff disapprovingly at the liquor fumes as she filled our plates with chicken-fried steak, corn on the cob, and red beans. Mrs. Sheriff was temperance.

Mostly the Sheriff helped me with military deserters. His help was not without a pecuniary motive. The Sheriff liked to collect the bounties paid for their apprehension by the military. Navy and Marine deserters were worth fifty dollars each, while army deserters were worth only twenty-five. For that reason the Sheriff would become much more excited about looking for a missing sailor or Marine than for an army man. "Wonder why the army has to be so chinchy," he would complain. "It all comes out of their own pay anyway." The Sheriff and I would go arrest them, and I would leave them in his jail so that he could call the military. As a federal officer I was not allowed to claim the rewards, but the sheriff could. We caught the same ones several times. There was a set of twins from the Sheriff's county who were continually stealing motorcycles and running off from the Marines. We apprehended them three times before the Marines finally gave up and handed them their dishonorable discharges.

"I made three hundred dollars in ree-wards on them twins and recovered six stolen motorsickles," the Sheriff bragged. "Them old boys was money-making dudes for this Sheriff. I was real sorry to see the Marines kick them out. They ain't been worth that much money to nobody else since."

"They wouldn't have been given that third chance if they hadn't been twins," I said.

"Yeah," said the Sheriff, "seems like twins always get

special treatment in this world. Guess it's because they are kind of a novelty."

One evening in his office, drinking bootleg whisky Cokes, I noticed what looked like a skinny yellow tree branch, about eighteen inches long, hanging on nails driven into the wall. I looked at it close. "What's that thing, Sheriff?"

We had had a fifty-dollar Navy deserter day, and the Sheriff was in a good mood. "I'll tell you if you promise not to tell nobody else. It's a bull's prick."

"A bull prick? You mean something you stick a bull with?"

"No, no, it's *his* prick. What he sticks into a cow. It's a dried, preserved bull's peter. Reason I don't want you telling everybody about it is because sometimes I have some fun with it."

I forgot about the bull's prick until later when I learned how he had fun with it.

During the time I was Mr. Hoover's personal representative on the Sparta road trip, a first-office agent named Marina, fresh from training school, transferred into our resident agency. After a short talk with him, the Senior Resident Agent said to me, "This guy has more nonessential, unimportant information at his fingertips than anyone I've ever met. His brain is a dustbin full of trivia. Also, he's a smart ass who needs the firm guidance of an experienced, older man. I am assigning him to help you on the Sparta road trip."

"Thanks," I said. The Senior Resident Agent wasn't doing me any favor. He was dropping Marina on me to keep him and his smart ass out of the office as much as possible.

Marina was from Cleveland and had graduated from Western Reserve University. I have never been to Cleveland, but if it in any way resembles the place he described, it combines the cultural grandeur of ancient Greece and the recreation facilities of Disneyland. Especially Shaker Heights. That was the Cleveland suburb he was from. He was a tall, loud young man who had played college basketball. He could not get it through his head that as a first-office agent he had no status at all until he did something outstanding, like catching a bank robber or shafting an inspector. His attitude was that everybody else had to prove themselves to him.

The first time I took Marina to Sparta with me was to cover a lead on an "IO Fugitive" case. "IO" stood for "Identification Order"—those white cards with photos and fingerprints you see on the walls of post offices. IOs were issued only on the more badly wanted fugitives. When I told Marina about the IO lead in Sparta, he said "Big deal" but condescended to go. After a couple of hours of 80-mile-an-hour driving in an easterly direction we arrived in Sparta in the middle of the afternoon and parked in one of the Sheriff's spaces on the courthouse square.

"Who's that, John Wayne?" Marina asked, looking at the statue of the Confederate cavalryman on the lawn. He walked over and read the inscription:

"Erected in Memory of Hood's Texas Brigade, Those Brave Men Who Lost Their Lives Valiantly Fighting for the Principle of States' Rights, as Guaranteed Under the Constitution of the United States, in the War for the Liberation of the Southern Confederacy, 1861–65."

"Jesus Christ! Where did they get that 'War for the Liberation of the Southern Confederacy'?"

"That's the real name of the Civil War. Didn't they teach you that at Western Reserve?"

"Jesus Christ!" he said.

We walked down the stairs to the basement office and found Daddy Frank. He was standing in the dimly

lighted hall in front of the Sheriff's office, a huge, forbidding figure. To my satisfaction Marina jumped back-
ward in fright, and I thought for a minute he was going
to panic and run up the steps and hide behind the statue.
I walked up to Daddy Frank, grabbed his hand, looked
into his good eye, and asked where the Sheriff was.
Daddy Frank said the Sheriff had taken the dogs out
early that morning to hunt for an escapee from one of
the state prison farms in the vicinity but had just called
in on the radio that he was on his way back. "We'll sit
out on the lawn and wait," I told Daddy Frank.

"Jesus Christ," said Marina, as we sat on a bench in
the shade. "What part does the big spook play in this
comedy? He looks like something Dr. Frankenstein put
together out of two or three Mandingos and Big Daddy
Lipscomb."

"Don't let the Sheriff hear you call Daddy Frank a
spook. He wouldn't like it."

"Daddy Frank? Is that his name? Jesus Christ!"

A few minutes later the Sheriff of Poindexter County
made his triumphal return to Sparta. He was driving his
souped-up Dodge sedan with three deputies inside, pulling a trailer that held Big Mama and three other mourn-
ful-looking bloodhounds. As he approached the square
he touched the siren button lightly, making it moan. The
moaning of the siren brought responsive howls from the
bloodhounds in the trailer. He circled the courthouse
twice, siren moaning and dogs howling, before parking
next to my FBI car.

"What kind of shit is that?" Marina asked.

"He's letting the voters know that the Sheriff of Poindexter County is on the job," I said.

"This is ridiculous," said Marina.

While the deputies unhitched the dog trailer, I told the
Sheriff what our mission was and showed him the IO

flyer. He held it out from his face like a man playing the trombone and studied the picture. "Yeah, that's old Bobby Jack Hardcastle all right. Pretty good likeness. He started off here holding up filling stations and a Piggly Wiggly store, and now he's graduated to banks, huh? His daddy's behind the Walls in Huntsville and his mama lives on the edge of town. The whole family is sorry as pig shit." He turned to the deputies and said, "You boys go on down and have some Cokes and bust-head. The Sheriff and these two FBIs is going out and talk to Bobby Jack Hardcastle's mama. We'll be back shortly."

The Sheriff stopped his car a few houses down the street from a small frame house on the edge of town. "That's old lady Hardcastle's place. You boys go to the front door and knock, and I'll sneak in the house through the back door. Last time I caught his daddy at home he was in the attic. There's a trap door in the kitchen ceiling."

Marina and I went up the front walk and I banged on the wall by the screen door. It was a warm day, so the inner door was open. I could see through the screen all the way to the back door. A lady in a cotton house dress and dirty pink house shoes shuffled to the door. "Yes?" she said. "What is it?" Over her shoulder I could see the Sheriff inserting what looked like a piece of wire through the mesh of the screen to lift the door hook.

I showed her my FBI credentials, told her who we were, asked her if she was the mother of Bobby Jack Hardcastle. She said she was. I told her there was a warrant out for Bobby Jack for bank robbery in Oklahoma. Mrs. Hardcastle rolled her eyes skyward as if to ask, "What else, Lord?" She said she had not seen her son in weeks and did not know where he was. Over her shoulder I could see the Sheriff ease the back door open, slip inside, and close the door soundlessly behind him.

I said, well, since Bobby Jack wasn't there, then of course she wouldn't object to our coming in and looking around a little so we could tell our boss man in Dallas that Bobby Jack's mother wasn't letting him stay at home. Well, she said, she didn't like to have strange men coming into her house, because you know how things were these days. Strange men were always getting into houses where women were alone and knocking them in the head and robbing them. Over her shoulder I could see a room almost bare of furniture and wondered what she had to steal. The Sheriff was setting up a tall kitchen stool in the middle of the kitchen.

Well, yes, I said, I could understand how she felt, all right, but after all we were law officers. I assured her I believed her when she said that her son wasn't there, but you know how these boss men were. I told her with a great deal of foreboding that if we went back to Dallas and told our boss man—

There was a crash and clatter inside the house, and Sheriff began yelling, "Get down from there, Bobby Jack. Let go up there, you hear me!"

We jerked the door open and rushed past Mrs. Hardcastle into the house. In the kitchen the Sheriff had hold of a man's leg protruding from a hole in the ceiling and was trying to pull the rest of the man out. The Sheriff was so short his feet were swinging off the floor. "Look out for the old lady. Frying pan!" he gasped.

I turned just in time to grab a heavy iron frying pan from the hands of Mrs. Hardcastle, who was about to crown the Sheriff with it. I pushed her out of the way.

"Little partner," the Sheriff gasped to Marina, "get on that stool and reach up there and grab him by the belt or the nuts or anything you can get aholt of and pull. I'm going to get him down from there if it hairlips everybody in Poindexter County."

Marina got up on the stool and reached up into the darkness. He must have grabbed something vital because there was a sudden scream and Hardcastle let go. The three of them—Hardcastle, Marina, and the sheriff—landed in the middle of the floor.

Something banged the side of my head and I saw a shower of bright flashes. The old lady had cracked me with a saucepan, luckily a small aluminum one. I slapped her across the room and tied her hands behind her back with her apron, but not before she bit me on the thumb. So I slapped her again and slammed her down in a chair. "Sit there!" I said.

The Sheriff and Marina now had Hardcastle flat on his face on the floor and were handcuffing him. After they searched him, the Sheriff handed Marina a flashlight hanging from his belt. "Little partner, how about you taking this light and going up into that attic and seeing what you can find."

Marina set up the stool and crawled up into the attic. When he came back covered with dust, he had a brown paper bag stuffed with currency and a blue steel .45 caliber automatic pistol.

"Aw Haw!" crowed the Sheriff triumphantly. He grabbed Hardcastle by the hair and jerked his head back. "Now, tell us where the car is, Bobby Jack. I know you got a getaway car around here somewhere and it's stolen."

"I ain't got no car," said Hardcastle.

"We'll talk more about that car at the jail," said the Sheriff. While Marina and I sat on Hardcastle in the kitchen and his mother remained in the chair staring impassively out the back door, the Sheriff prowled through the house whistling softly to himself. He returned in a few minutes carrying an old single-barrel 12-gauge shotgun. "I'm taking this along for your own

good, Mrs. Hardcastle, so it won't tempt you to do anything rash." As we hustled her handcuffed son toward
the door, the Sheriff said to her, "If you ever attack
another officer when he's in your house on official bidness, Mrs. Hardcastle, I'm going to lock you up. You
hear me, Mrs. Hardcastle?"

"When my man gets out of the pen, he's going to be
looking for you, Sheriff."

"That won't be for another six years, Mrs. Hardcastle,
so don't get your hopes up. If he talks to them farm cap-
tains the way he talks to people around here, he won't
make it. He won't be looking for anything but a cool
spot in hell."

When we got back to the jail, the Sheriff and Marina
fingerprinted and photographed Hardcastle. Then, while
the Sheriff had a private interview with him, Marina
came back to the office where, as part of his training, I
showed him how to write a glowing teletype describing
how he and I captured this badly wanted Bureau fugitive
singlehandedly with the Sheriff standing by as a mere
witness. I explained the Sheriff's presence by saying he
knew Hardcastle by sight. "That is a very important
point," I said.

"What?"

"That the Sheriff was merely there as a witness. When
you apprehend a Bureau fugitive and a police officer
helps you, you have to explain why he was there in the
first teletype to the Bureau and play down his role, or
you may get your ass racked. The Director won't tolerate local officers mollycoddling agents. You have to say
who all was there, and if a local officer was present you
have to give a logical explanation."

"Isn't it enough to arrest the guy and put him in jail?"

"Oh, hell no. That's generally the simplest part of it.
You've got to put just exactly the right information in

the apprehension teletype. Leave out anything that the Director might not want to hear. If he doesn't like the way you caught somebody it's worse than not catching the guy at all."

"Jesus Christ," said Marina. "It would be simpler just to sit in the office and never to catch anybody."

"A lot of agents have figured that out," I said.

When the Sheriff came back to the office, he was still whistling tunelessly between his teeth, the way he did when things were going his way. "Old Bobby Jack let down his milk about that getaway car," he said. "There's a new Chevy sedan hid out in a barn near his mama's house that he stole off a car dealer's lot in Duncan, Oklahoma, after the bank robbery. I just sent a wrecker after it." The Sheriff kept on whistling. A new Chevy was worth at least a fifty-dollar ransom from the dealer.

While I was counting the money from the paper bag, labeling the pistol as evidence, and finishing up the paper work, Marina got a chance to tell the Sheriff all about Cleveland and Shaker Heights and Western Reserve University and how he was a big shot basketball player who had almost been drafted by several professional teams.

The Sheriff was impressed. "Gee whiz, little partner, you'll have to go down and shoot some goals at our new high school gym. You might could give the coach some ideas. He's also the high school principal and don't have a lot of time to spend with the team. You might come down for some of the games during the basketball season. You could probably sit on the bench."

Marina did not seem overwhelmed by the invitation. He spoke disparagingly of basketball as played anywhere but in the Midwest. He said the crudity of the play of any Texas basketball teams would just irritate and embarrass him.

Daddy Frank and a couple of deputies came in, accompanied by the County Attorney, a gangling young man with the dark suit and melancholy air of an undertaker, taller than Marina but skinnier.

The Sheriff introduced the County Attorney to Marina. "He played basketball at Baylor University in Waco and almost lettered," the Sheriff said.

Marina then gave his expert opinion that the basketball as played in the Southwestern Conference was of very poor quality.

"It's the South*west* Conference, not the Southwestern Conference," said the Sheriff. "I can always spot a poor quality, uninformed Yankee sports commentator who don't know his butt about the world of sports, when he calls it the Southwestern Conference."

"Well, whatever you call it, the basketball played here has no quality," said Marina. "The only place you can see good basketball is in the Midwest."

"What part of the Midwest is UCLA in?" the County Attorney asked.

Well, the fact that UCLA had won several national basketball championships was just a freak accident, according to Marina. It hinged on the fact that a lot of good spook players wanted to live in California because they knew they could screw the white women out there.

The Sheriff brought Cokes from the machine in the hall and dug out a bottle of bourbon. Big Mama drank her ration of Coke from the plastic bowl, sneezed violently, and farted.

Marina, drinking his Coke without dilution because he was still in training in the hope he would be drafted by a professional basketball team, gagged and waved his handkerchief around in front of his face. "God Almighty!" he said. "What a stink! What do you feed that damn hound? Old rubber tires?"

"Don't nobody strike a match in here," the Sheriff said. "This place would explode. Daddy Frank, get her out into the hall before we suffocate."

Daddy Frank picked up the big hound as though she was a puppy and carried her out.

Marina took a pull on his Coke. "Well, Sheriff, I'd say you got a real armpit town here."

There was a silence as we all sipped our Cokes and thought over that observation.

The County Attorney said, "I'm glad you went into the FBI instead of the State Department. You might have been sent to Russia and precipitated a nuclear attack."

Marina did not dignify that observation with a response.

Finally the Sheriff said, "It's not so bad in the spring, when the lemon trees are in bloom."

"Lemon trees?" That caught Marina's attention. He had taken a course in forestry at Western Reserve and knew all about trees. "I haven't seen any lemon trees around here."

"We have a lot of them," said the Sheriff.

"Bullshit," said Marina. "I would have noticed any lemon trees around here."

The Sheriff bobbed his head at the wall.

"There's a switch I cut from a lemon tree up there on those deer horns."

Marina stood up and took the thin yellow switch from the horns. He held it to his nose and sniffed it. "It doesn't smell like lemon wood to me."

"Lemon wood, after it's dried out, don't smell much," the Sheriff explained. "If you bite it, you can get a lemony taste."

Marina put the thin stick in his mouth and bit it carefully, then smacked his lips. "It doesn't taste like lemon to me."

"Bite it harder," said the Sheriff. "The taste will come through."

Marina put the stick in his mouth so that it stuck out from side to side like a dog fetching a newspaper and chomped down hard. "Uh shtill cuh tate enny emmon," he said between clenched teeth.

"What?" asked the Sheriff.

Marina removed the stick from his mouth. "I said I still can't taste any lemon."

"What does it taste like?" the Sheriff asked.

"Nothing," said Marina. "It doesn't taste like anything at all to me, except it's a little salty."

"I guess they don't have lemon wood up there in the Midwest," said the Sheriff.

"No," said Marina, his face reddening stubbornly, "but I've studied forestry at Western Reserve and I've seen lemon wood trees in California." He sniffed away at the stick like Big Mama sniffing an escapee's shoe and bit it a couple of more times. "You know," he said finally, "I do get a sort of lemony taste along with the salt, now that you mention it."

"Maybe that old bull ate a lemon before they conked him on the head at the packing house," said the County Attorney.

Marina looked at the stick, mystified. "What do you mean?"

"That's a petrified bull's prick you're chewing on," said the County Attorney.

Marina threw the stick to the floor, washed his mouth out with Coke, spat it out in the lavatory. "You told me it was lemon wood."

"I guess if somebody told you Jesus Christ was born under an apple tree, you'd believe that too," the County Attorney said.

9

Sacking the SACs

He would look through his telescope from the heights of SOG and see the SACs and ASACs as mere specks in the sky over Denver or Miami or St. Louis and would carefully aim his SAM missile. "I've got him in my sights, Clyde."

And Clyde would say, "Perhaps a few degrees to the left, Eddie."

And Eddie would say, "I never go left, I always go right, Clyde."

And Clyde would say, "You know best, Eddie."

And Eddie would push the button or pull the trigger or whatever you do to fire a SAM, and the rocket would whiz skyward and crash into the speck in the sky over Denver or Miami or St. Louis. Then there would be a screeching, falling sound culminating in a loud thump. And there on the bricks would be a SAC or an ASAC, heat shield burned to a cinder, eyebrows scorched, and eyes glazed.

"You thought you were riding high, in permanent orbit, didn't you?" the Director would ask.

"*Yes,*" *said the victim groggily.* "*What did I do wrong?*"

"*Well,*" *said the Director,* "*you were becoming complacent, that's what. I shot you down for your own good. A little slap on the wrist never hurt anybody.*"

"*Why, you senile old—*"

"*Now, now,*" *said the Director.* "*You aren't a veteran, are you? You must be temporarily deranged to talk to me like that. Aren't you?*"

"*I guess so.*"

"*Well, repeat after me. 'I must have been temporarily deranged to say that about my beloved Director.'* "

"*I must have been temporarily deranged to say that about my beloved Director.*"

"*Now, say, 'a little slap on the wrist never hurt anybody.'* "

"*A little slap on the wrist never . . .*"

Oh, those SACs! They fascinated me—their quirks, their foibles, their fears, their whimsies, their pretensions. They were so ambitious, yet so fearful; so ego-driven, yet so hesitant and vulnerable. They had so many dreams, generally inflated with hot air. Some reminded me of Richard Burton reading the lines from *Camelot* that tell how he had become King. The scene was re-enacted many times at SOG. An ambitious young supervisor, naught but a mere squire, would be galloping along on a sorry nag dreaming about how he could help his Director in the holy war currently being waged against Knoxville. Passing through a park, he noticed a sword imbedded in a stone. "Some sort of war memorial," he thought, "but my Director needs all the swords he can get to battle the uncircumcised trolls of Knoxville." Clothed in samite incorruptible, he strode up to the stone and grasped the hilt. Lo, the sword turned in his hand

and came free of the stone. As he brandished it above his head, a great crowd of SOG supervisors appeared from nowhere, cheering and shouting, "Arthur! Arthur! King of Knoxville!"

Then he made his triumphant flight to Knoxville, leaving his wife to sell the house in Silver Spring and do the dirty work. He was on a holy mission for the Director. He was the Director's personal representative. "Were it not so," the Director had intoned, "I would not tell you. You are going to Knoxville as my personal representative, not to mollycoddle agents." He had been briefed by the assistant directors on the gigantic problems of ruling Knoxville, and now he was on his way, his balls aflame with the desire to screw every agent who got in his way, for the glory of the Director.

He rolled out of bed every morning at 5 A.M. to be the first to sign in on the Number One register at the office. He made Bureau speeches—breakfasts, lunches, dinners, Optimists, Kiwanians, Rotarians, Lions. At night he addressed PTA meetings, Boy Scouts, church groups —always preaching the message of the Director. He sent in a continual stream of memos telling the Director how he was bringing the good news to the cannibals, to use the words of Mark Twain.

Then came the time for the first inspection. Arthur tried to build his employees up to a high pitch of efficiency: clean the walls, clean the desks, clean the filing cabinets! Get the cases posted! Get the old charge-out slips out of the files! Go! Go!

The inspector and his staff appeared. Somehow the inspector looked vaguely familiar, darkly menacing, a secret smile, a slightly spraddle-legged walk, as though his balls were as hot and fragile as turned-on 100-watt light bulbs.

"Who does this guy remind me of?" Arthur mur-

mured to himself. "Why does he look so familiar?" Then one day in a wave of introspective melancholy, after the inspector had called him to his office, smiling a secret triumphant smile, to show him some files in which he had found subs, it came to Arthur. "My God, he reminds me of me! Me, a year ago. Back when I was still dreaming the dream. He's the Enemy."

And the Enemy said, "Arthur, it looks like you've let the administration go to pot around here. I am going to have to write up these subs. Nothing personal, you understand. Just part of the job."

And Arthur almost screamed, "Subs! What about all my speeches? What about all my liaison contacts? What about all the sermons I've preached spreading the gospel of St. Edgar?"

So after the inspector wrote up the subs and a number of sacrificial goats were burned at the altar, Arthur got a nasty letter cataloguing his failures and weaknesses and summoning him to SOG for an audience with the Director. The Director kept Arthur waiting in the front office interminably, notebook in hand, chewing his fingernails, talking with Sam Noisette, the black special agent who was the Director's doorman.

Noisette was an artist. His paintings often hung on display in the Director's front office. Arthur, like other SACs, bought one of his paintings as he sweated there, just for luck. Arthur cared nothing for art, but Noisette seemed to have the Director's affection since he had survived so long at such close quarters with him. He might be able to put in a good word some way.

Arthur finally got in to see The Man and took his blast. Since the charges were serious, he got a good one. When he stumbled out, he was on probation and could expect another office inspection within ninety days. When he touched base with the assistant directors, they talked to him in guarded tones, and only in the presence of witnesses, treating him as though he had a contagious disease. Even his rabbi acted aloof, trying to find an excuse for not going to lunch. He finally agreed to go but suggested an out-of-the-way place. There they huddled in a booth, and Arthur poured out his woes to his rabbi, while the rabbi kept looking over his shoulder and saying, "Kind of keep your voice down, Arthur, won't you? Try not to get so excited. I'll do what I can. But you know I've got to protect myself too."

Then Arthur went back to his field office and every time the Bureau telephone rang he jumped as though someone had slyly tweaked his genitalia. He was waiting, waiting for the drop of the second shoe—the appearance of the inspectors.

One day he received a long distance call. It was from his rabbi at SOG. "Arthur, I'm calling from a pay booth at the bus station, because I don't want this going through the switchboard at the B. You're going to have visitors tomorrow and there's a contract out for you."

"C-contract? Are you sure?"

"Yeah," said the rabbi, "The dominant theme is 'misplaced confidence.' "

"Muh-misplaced confidence?"

"Well, shit, Arthur, you don't think the Old Man is going to admit he made a mistake in promoting you in the first place, do you? Let's not be naïve. He says he trusted you with an assignment and you let him down. You know, 'misplaced confidence.' " Then the rabbi hung up.

Instead of mobilizing the troops to blitz the filing cabinets, walls, and desks, Arthur went out and got plastered.

The goons flew in next day and for the next week or so it was Custer's Last Stand all over again. This time the Indians had AR-15s instead of bows and arrows and F-111s for air support. Arthur stood on his little mound of high ground chopping back at the painted savages with his singing sword and ducking the bombs that rained on him from heaven.

"I give him credit," said one of the agents from that office later, "Arthur really fought back. He found where some of the goons were having a drinking party one night after work and when they left the place driving a rented car, he had them arrested for DWI. He fired that off to the Bureau and that got the senior inspector chewed out and the three aides busted. Then he had a stroke of pure luck. One of the girls from the steno pool came to Arthur privately and told him that one of the young aides had patted her on the butt and tried to make a date with her. She also said that another of the aides had propositioned one of the other girls in the office. The steno wanted to know what to do. Arthur was delighted to tell her. 'It is our duty to inform the Director!' he said. Arthur knew that both those aides were married, and this little escapade would finish them off as far as the Director was concerned. He marched both girls in to confer with the senior inspector. The senior inspector turned pale when he heard the news, but he tried to play it down. Boys will be boys. My God, this might blow *his* career out of the tub!

"Arthur picked up the telephone and called the assistant director in charge of the Inspection Division personally, displaying the reckless courage of someone with absolutely nothing to lose. 'These inspectors of yours are trying to turn my office into a whorehouse,' he yelled at the assistant director. 'This is the worst example of misplaced confidence I have ever seen. I can't even get the senior inspector to do his duty.'

"The assistant director said he would be down on the next plane. He instructed the senior inspector and the two fanny slappers to stay in the office until he got there, no matter how late his plane came in. It was after midnight before he arrived, and by then Arthur had obtained signed statements from his two stenographers describing the lewd and lascivious advances of the two aides. The senior inspector, smelling sulphur in the wind, took detailed confessions from his two sex fiends.

"After the assistant director had read the statements, he called in the two aides and asked in a disarming, jovial fashion what their offices of preference were. One of them said New York and the other said Los Angeles. 'Fine,' he said, 'the one who wants to go to New York will go to Los Angeles and the one who wants Los Angeles will go to New York, and you will probably stay there for the rest of your natural lives as far as the Bureau is concerned. If you want to resign here and now that's O.K. with me.'

" 'When do we have to go?' one of them asked.

" 'Next plane,' said the assistant director.

" 'What about our families?' one asked.

" 'That's your problem,' said the assistant director, 'but you are *not* to go back to Washington for any reason until given permission.' They took off in opposite directions that night. God only knows what they told their wives."

"What about Arthur?"

"Oh, Arthur came out of it smelling like Arpège. The Director decided that a guy with his talent was being wasted in a field office so he was promoted to Number One man in the Inspection Division at SOG. The assistant director is scared shitless of him, of course. I understand there's a ray of light from above that shines down on his head all the time. All the supervisors are afraid of him too. They hug the wall when he passes by. They're afraid he'll unsheath his singing sword."

Arthur was one of the fantastically lucky ones who dodged the missile. Most of the time it hit dead center, and the busted SAC landed kerthump on the bricks of the field office selected by the blindfolded chimpanzee. There, the object of the snickers of the hardhearted, he was a pitiful sight to behold. Distrusted and shunned by the Field agents who may have suffered at his hands during his fleeting days of power, he would crouch in a corner like a fallen eagle, tail feathers burned off by the rocket blast, thumbing through the heavy, black-bound manuals, trying to relearn how to investigate cases. Some, harboring desperate hopes of reinstatement, held whispered conversations with erstwhile friends and rabbis at SOG, plotting schemes for again scaling the heights and being restored to the bosom of the Director. The schemes generally failed. The Director was an unforgiving god. Once a SAC had failed him, the wretch, as a rule, was doomed to wander the Field for the rest of his days.

"It took a hell of an effort to throw off the covers and get up every morning after they sent me down to Mobile on the bricks," one of them told me once. "I was in my late forties and had too much time invested to get out. 'If I could just get in to see the Director,' I would think to myself, 'I could explain it.' But I couldn't seem to get in. Maybe Mr. Tolson or Miss Gandy had poisoned his mind against me. Finally I decided that life was too short to spend it trying to brown-nose the Old Man. I decided the only mark I was ever going to make in the Bureau was to write my name on a field office rest room wall, so to hell with it. I began looking after the young agents who I could see were heading for trouble and advising those in trouble how to get out. A sort of jailhouse lawyer, see? I get a kind of kick out of screwing the Bureau at its own game. I guess you might say I developed the mentality of a Field agent."

"Did you lose much money?"

"Oh, hell, I lost six, seven thousand dollars a year, but the worst thing about being busted isn't the money. The worst thing is what happens to you in the eyes of your family. 'What did you do wrong?' they ask. 'I didn't do anything wrong,' you answer. 'You must have done something wrong or Mr. Hoover wouldn't have demoted you,' they say. You can't ever explain it. It's your word against his, even in your own family. It's a hell of a blow to your pride. When you're first promoted, you always think getting busted is something that happens to somebody else. Now it's happened to you. You lose faith in yourself. The things that used to be true aren't true any more. Everything has turned to stone. I don't think Mr. Hoover really understood this phase of his disciplinary actions because he never had a family—wife and kids, I mean. But then, on the other hand, maybe he did, and that was a planned part of his punishment."

"I would like to say something about the chair you had to sit in, in the Director's office, and also about the way the Director's desk was situated," said one former ASAC who had been shot down at such low altitude his sense of humor had not been seriously damaged in the crash. "The Director was sort of short, see, so he had his chair and desk raised some way so that no matter how tall you were, you were always below his eye level when you sat in front of his desk. The chair had a pneumatic cushion with a very slow air leak. As you sat there, you felt yourself slowly, slowly sinking, until he seemed to tower over you as you tried to look up at him between your knees and write in that goddam notebook. After a few minutes in that chair, if you were as tall and skinny as I am, you felt like a stork trying to sit in a water bucket."

One Irish Catholic, broken from SAC after a stormy tirade from Mr. Hoover, told me, "I think it would be more appropriate to have an altar rail there in front of his desk instead of a chair. Then the penitent could kneel there and say the Rosary or sing hymns and yell, 'Amen!' every time the old bastard paused for breath, which was not often."

There's a hypersensitive Irishman for you. Everything had been going fine for him in Boston until something he said at a communion breakfast irritated Boston's aged resident Cardinal.

"I stood up, after a couple of Bloody Marys, and made the old remark that's been made around the Bureau about a million times that all good Irish Catholic boys from Boston either became priests or FBI agents. I didn't make it up. I don't know who did. But in my speech, I attributed the remark to the Director. Everybody clapped and laughed. One of the priests who was there mentioned it to the Cardinal and he took offense. The Cardinal wrote a letter to the Director warning him to beware of making 'sacrilegious remarks.' Jesus, did the Old Man take me apart! 'I never made that stupid remark!' he kept hollering at me. 'What other lies have you put into my mouth?' And I kept sinking lower and lower into that chair."

"What was your penance?"

"Three years in Detroit on the bricks. Then he sent me to New Haven. 'I will never send you back to Boston,' he said when he gave me the New Haven transfer. 'I will never send you back to Boston.' And he never did."

Some of the broken ones required psychiatric help. Like many people in that predicament, they did not realize it at first until it was explained to them. When one SAC was busted because one of his agents in a distant resident agency did something reprehensible over which the SAC had no control, the SAC snarled, "That senile old son of a bitch!" referring, of course, to the Director. The inspector who had heard the remark put it into his report, but luckily the SAC's rabbi at SOG caught the report and wrote on it, "Psychiatry obviously required. Shock must have temporarily deranged him." The rabbi knew that the only way to save the guy's job after that outburst was to plead insanity. The rabbi called the bustee's new SAC and told him that the fallen man must be examined by a psychiatrist immediately, and the diagnosis had to be "temporary derangement" or something like that.

The busted SAC was sent to a psychiatrist at a government hospital, and the opinion came back that his remarks had been the result of a "normal outburst of uncontrollable anger." His new SAC improved on that by changing it to "an *abnormal* outburst of *temporarily* uncontrollable anger *at himself due to frustration at being unable to meet the Director's high standards of performance*." That seemed to satisfy the god of Olympus, and the former SAC was allowed to fade into the crowd, becoming another field office nonentity.

Some of the busted ones reacted in unique ways. One ASAC who was busted at Cincinnati and sent to New Orleans on the bricks would never admit he had been busted. "I have merely been reassigned," he would say, angrily. He had been reassigned all right—vertically downward. I have read there are Russian prisoners in Siberia who deny the obvious fact they are prisoners. "We are citizens on file," they say.

"Do you consider yourself an ASAC on file?" I asked him.

"I consider you a sarcastic son of a bitch," he said and stormed out of the bar where he had allowed me to buy the drinks for old times' sake.

Some time ago I saw in a news story that Director Clarence Kelley of the FBI was instituting a system of "participatory management" within the FBI. As part of that program he was inviting three or four SACs to Kansas City every weekend for eyeball-to-eyeball conversation about what was actually going on in the Field. I don't know if this procedure is productive or not. It is a logical course for Mr. Kelley to pursue since, as a former SAC, he must be aware that a form of life exists in the Field and occasionally something of value can be learned from listening to a SAC—provided, of course, the SAC can be induced to tell the truth about what actually goes on.

If Mr. Hoover had attempted this, any SAC ordered to appear would have been scared witless. He would go through a frantic spell of mental inventory, trying to recall all the things that might be wrong with his office. He was not going to confess them. He was going to try to hide them. If Mr. Hoover already had the goods on him, the SAC would try to justify whatever it was he had done or failed to do by blaming someone else.

Then the SAC would worry about his clothes; he would tell his wife to make sure he had new white shirts, black socks, and somber neckties. Then he would robe himself in a conservative dark suit and carry a spare one in a hanger bag, just in case a pigeon crapped on him somewhere between the airport and the place where he was going to see Mr. Hoover. Once in the presence of the Director he would sit hunched slightly forward with notebook in lap to record the revealed word.

All he would say was what he thought the Director wanted to hear, whether it was true or not. The SAC knew that if he told Mr. Hoover what actually went on in the Field, he would be busted because he would have to tell the Old Man that the magic rules did not work. People got in the way. Mr. Hoover certainly would not tolerate one of his personal representatives letting people (Bureau people) get in the way of getting things done. Bureau people were supposed to do what they were told.

So the SAC would not participate. He would listen. He would take copious notes in his notebook. He would nod. He would murmur, "Yes, yes, Mr. Hoover." But he would not participate by revealing any of the real problems of the Field, because to do so would be fatal to his career.

10

"You Gotta Have Stats, Miles and Miles and Miles of Stats..."

The words in the title above should be sung very loudly to the tune of "You Gotta Have Heart" from the Broadway show Damn Yankees *by every SAC in the Bureau to the assembled employees of his office every morning immediately after he has drawn the line and initialed the Number 1 Register, after the last employee has signed in.*

It was always poor policy for a headquarters city agent to live in the same neighborhood as his SAC. For one thing, if the SAC was strict and imbued with his importance as the Director's personal representative, the agent had to be very careful about bringing his Bureau car home—a serious breach of the Director's rules. A truly dedicated SAC might take a late evening stroll past his house and even peek into his garage to see if a Bureau car was hidden there. On the other hand, if the SAC was the devil-may-care type—and there were a few of those around, believe it or not—he might encourage the agent to take his Bureau car home, with the stipulation that the agent had to drive him to work in the morning and home at night. Thus, the agent became the SAC's personal chauffeur. He had to rise early and pick up the SAC in the morning, and he could not leave the office at night until the SAC was finished, which might be late. Furthermore, if the SAC received an urgent phone call in the middle of the night to dispatch an agent somewhere on some unpleasant task, he knew where one was available with a Bureau car.

Also, I have heard on the grapevine that some SACs had a penchant for drafting agents to do house repairs, build fences and patios, mow lawns, and clip hedges. I never worked for a SAC like that, to my knowledge. I say "to my knowledge" because I spent most of my career in a resident agency, geographically separated from the headquarters city, so I never had a neighborhood acquaintanceship with any of the SACs I worked for.

Unquestionably, if you lived near your SAC and became close friends, you would have to share his sorrows and joys, and SACs generally had more sorrows than anything else.

Take the case of B. D. Boggs and his SAC, Elmer Earwood, an example of the dangers inherent in an agent's living near his SAC. B.D., Earwood, and I had gone through New Agents together. B.D. and I had been brand-new, but Elmer had been a retread. He had served five years in the Bureau as an agent, mostly as a supervisor at SOG, prior to entering military service in World War II. He decided it would help him later in life to have served in the military, so he put on the suit for a while—the military suit, that is. Earwood quit the Bureau in 1944 and joined the Marines for a year or so. After discharge, on the strength of his military record, he tried his hand at politics, unsuccessfully running for

county attorney in his home town. Then he tried prac-
ticing law, but few clients appeared. He decided he was
getting nowhere, suit or no suit, so he reapplied for a
job with the Bureau and was welcomed by the Director
as a prodigal son. However, the Director made him go
through New Agents again as a toll to be paid for his
temporary disloyalty. For some reason the Director
marked Earwood for advancement. His X-ray eye apparently detected some sterling trait or quality in Earwood
not visible to the eye of a mere mortal. I avoided him
in New Agents because my delicate patrician nostrils
detected about him the faint odor of finkdom. Perhaps
the qualities that the Director's X-ray eye and my patrician nose had detected were the same.

One night, when a bunch from the class were whoop-
ing it up, drinking beer after hours at the River View
Hotel in Quantico, the SAC from the Academy appeared
and took all their names, getting them all letters of
censure with which to launch their Bureau careers.
Luckily, I had wearied of the revelry and departed early.
When I signed the register at the Academy just before
curfew I noticed Earwood in the SAC's office making
a telephone call. Maybe there was no connection between that call and the River View raid. Maybe.

Earwood was promoted to ASAC of a field office
shortly after leaving New Agents for the Field. Then
he was promoted to SAC of still another office. This was
before the dangerous, winding path through the Jungle
of Goondom had been hacked out for those who desired
to rise in the Bureau. In those days the Director might
make one of his lightning decisions and elevate an agent
from the bricks to SAC in one electrifying goose.

Within a few years Earwood turned up as the SAC
of the office to which B. D. Boggs was assigned. By this
time the dew seems to have dried from the blossoming

rose of Earwood's career. His latest transfer had been from a larger office to one significantly smaller. In moments of introspection he experienced a melancholy premonition that all was not well. His career seemed to have peaked out and started downhill after his rabbi, an assistant director, had retired and gone to well-earned oblivion in Florida. When Elmer called the Bureau on the telephone these days people up there acted cool and disinterested in his problems. The new assistant director who had replaced his rabbi apparently had enough protégés of his own already and was not interested in increasing his herd.

Earwood bought a home in the same neighborhood as his old classmate B. D. Boggs and immediately formed a two-man car pool with him. B.D. was a good-natured, trusting guy who had been one of Earwood's few friends in New Agents. When I had divulged my suspicions regarding Earwood's possible finkdom in the River View beer-drinking incident, B.D. came to his defense and even impugned *my* motives. "You just can't stand to see anyone play the game by the rules," he said. "And you can't tolerate a winner."

"I don't think Elmer's much of a winner," I said. "I think he's a stool pigeon. Furthermore, I suspect he's the one the SAC had check the sign-out register that time I got into trouble about going to the movies. He was always snooping around the sign-out register. Every night."

"Envy," said B.D. "Just plain old envy. You don't have what it takes yourself to succeed in this outfit so you try to destroy someone who does. You're just trying to hang a stool pigeon label on Elmer. He may be a big man in this outfit some day."

So B.D. was overjoyed at the opportunity to car pool with his buddy, Earwood. At first. They used B.D.'s personal car because Earwood was afraid to take a Bureau car home. B.D. noticed at once that his old classmate had lost what little *joie de vivre* he'd previously had, back when he had basked in the ray of light from above. Now he seemed to live under an ever thickening cloud of apprehension. He stayed in the office late, fumbling through files, afraid to leave because someone from the Bureau might call and find him gone. He always went to the office early in the morning because someone might call before he got there and criticize him for that. He was afraid to leave the office for any reason, generally eating his meals at his desk. When the telephone calls from SOG did come he was quick to impress on the caller that he was in his office, had been there for hours, and would remain there until late that night.

"Elmer tried to supervise every case in the office," B.D. told me later. "He didn't trust the ASAC or the supervisor to do anything right. Everything was a major problem, even an applicant investigation. Every time we apprehended a fugitive—even a deserter—he wanted to call the B. personally to report the victory. But no matter what he did or how long he stayed in the office, he couldn't raise the stat level above the year before—in convictions, fugitives, cars recovered, and fines, savings, and recoveries. You see, we had had an unusually good year just before he transferred in. He became very nervous and lost his temper about the least thing. Missing a deserter would send him into a hysterical fit. On the way home at night he would sit in the car all hunched over like an old man, and sometimes in the morning on the way to work I would have to pull over to the curb so he could open the door and throw up his breakfast. I would say to him, 'My God, Elmer, life's too short for you to live it this way. Relax.'

"And he would just look at me and say, 'Relax, hell.

The stats are down. You know what that means? The stats are down. When the inspectors come in here, I'm cooked. They'll stack my ass as sure as hell. The last time I was in for a conference the Director chewed me out for low stats and Mr. Tolson was very cold, very cold. The other assistant directors were like icebergs. There's a contract out for me, sure as hell.' "

Then the day arrived. An inspector called from the airport for a ride into town. He said that the rest of the inspection team would be there the following morning.

Earwood had his trusted friend B. D. Boggs drive him to the airport to pick up the inspector. Earwood was squirming around in the seat thinking of all the secret things wrong at the office. "They didn't give me even a day's warning," he kept saying. "Not a day. When Stan was there, he always called me a couple of days ahead. Now he's down there in Florida fishing for tarpon and just screwing the dog." Stan had been his rabbi at SOG.

"All the way back to the hotel with the inspector, Elmer kept on babbling like a goddam idiot," B.D. said. "Mainly about how he couldn't get a goddam thing done because of the poor attitude of the investigative personnel. He said that the ASAC and supervisor weren't carrying their load and God knows what else. It sounded like he was trying to push off on them everything that could possibly go wrong during the inspection.

"The inspector, who really didn't seem like a bad guy, said, 'Relax, Elmer, the name of the game this year is stats. Just stats. The Old Man has to go before the House Appropriations Committee before long to ask for next year's money. If you're up in stats, there's no sweat.' "

B.D. and the SAC drove the inspector to his hotel, got him checked in, and made reservations for the other members of the goon squad who would arrive next day.

"I'm going to hit the sack early," said the inspector. "See you guys in the morning."

Driving home, B.D. said to Elmer, "He seemed like a pretty good guy."

Earwood sat hunched over as though his guts had turned to mush. "Did you hear what he said about stats?" When they reached his house, Earwood got out of the car without a word and went into his house.

Next morning when B.D. came by to pick him up at 6 A.M., the usual time, he was surprised that the SAC was not waiting out front for him. Generally Earwood was pacing up and down the sidewalk impatiently when B.D. drove up. B.D. beeped his horn discreetly. A minute or two later the front door opened, a head festooned with hair curlers appeared, and an arm beckoned. B.D. went up the walk to the front door. Mrs. Earwood stood there in a housecoat.

"Elmer won't get out of bed, B.D." she said. "I think he's sick or lost his mind. He's lying there with the cover up over his face and says he can't get out of bed because the stats are down."

B.D. followed Mrs. Earwood into the bedroom. Sure enough, there was a long, inert, mummy-like lump in the bed, covered from head to foot. B.D. raised the covers from the head end and said, "What's the matter, Elmer? Are you sick?"

Elmer glared up at B.D. and his wife. "Can't a man have any privacy even in his own bedroom? Of course I'm sick. I've been sick ever since Stan retired. I'm having to hang in and shovel shit while he fishes for tarpon down there in Florida and screws the dog."

"Elmer!" Mrs. Earwood gave him a shocked look and left the room.

Earwood pulled the sheet back over his face and went on talking in a muffled voice. "Let her go down there and explain about the stats, she's so goddam smart. That bastard in Florida sent me a picture of himself and a fish he'd caught the other day. That goddam fish must have been six feet long. And Stan was there grinning without a care in the world. He got me promoted to this lousy job and then ran off and left me hanging up like that goddam fish."

"Aw, come on, Elmer," said B.D. "You have to go to work."

"No," said Elmer through the sheet. "I'm sick."

Every morning for the next week B.D. stopped by Earwood's house on his way to work. He no longer honked. He just got out of the car and walked up to the door, Mrs. Earwood let him in, and he went into the bedroom. The scene was always the same. The muffled voice would say through the sheet, "I'm sick."

After three or four days Mrs. Earwood said, "He won't shave or bathe. He's beginning to smell bad. He won't let me change the sheets. I've moved into the guest room."

Feeling like a traitor, B.D. told the inspector. The inspector went to Earwood's house with B.D. and had a conversation with him through the bed sheet. "I'm a sick man," was all Elmer would say. "I got sick after Stan went to Florida."

Back at the office, the inspector said to his chief aide, "The stats here aren't really too bad for an office this size but you can't tell Earwood that. I'm afraid he's gone off his rocker. All he wants to talk about is that ex-rabbi of his who betrayed him by retiring to Florida. I'm going to have to call the B. but I can't tell the Old Man about the rabbi business. I'll just say he's had a nervous breakdown from overwork." A couple of days later, the inspector handed B.D. a sealed envelope addressed to Earwood from the Director. "Take this out and give it to him. For your private information it says he's being reduced to the bricks and sent to Phoenix for physical disabilities. No suspension, no probation, no disciplinary action. All for reasons of health, see? The new SAC will arrive this afternoon."

B.D. made his trip to Earwood's home, stood over the shrouded form, and announced he had a letter. A dirty hand appeared to carry the letter under the sheet. B.D. turned on the lamp by the bed. A few seconds later Earwood sat up and got out from under the covers. He had a week's growth of beard and smelled like a goat. He staggered into the bathroom, and soon B.D. could hear the muffled sound of water running in the bathtub. B.D. sat in the living room and waited. Mrs. Earwood appeared with the letter in her hand. "I think he just got well," she said, "and I did too."

Earwood appeared in the living room, hair combed, shaved, wearing a well-pressed suit. "Let's not screw around all day, B.D." he said, "We've got to get on down to the office."

Elmer cleaned his stuff out of the SAC's office while the new SAC, who had just arrived, thumbed through the inspector's report. "What about this drop in stats?" he asked.

"That's your problem," said Elmer.

A few minutes later the ASAC came in and asked Elmer, "Who's going to handle the speeches you're scheduled to make next week?"

"That's your problem," Elmer said.

That was the way it was the rest of the day. Elmer had no more problems. The faithful B.D. loaded Elmer's personal gear into the car and took it to his house. After he unloaded the car, Earwood said to him, "My wife and I are moving out next week and the new SAC is taking over this place. He's got his family in a motel right now. He wants to car pool with you."

"Bullshit!" said B.D.

"That's your problem," said Earwood. "I'm going down to the desert and lie in the sun, like Stan does on the beach at Tarpon Springs."

"You were right about him," B.D. told me later. "It's just like Jugbutt Queensland used to say. He tracked it all over me while I was there, and before he ran off he threw it at me."

11

The Genie in the Bottle

Most of the SACs I knew were dedicated, striving men who never, never openly criticized the Director about anything. But occasionally a maverick came along, one who was unique, whose success was a source of puzzlement to me. One of these mavericks was Herby the Schizo. I called him that because the easiest way to explain some of his actions was to say he had a split personality. Maybe his personality wasn't split at all. Maybe he was possessed of an evil spirit like the little girl in *The Exorcist* who did the dirty tricks with the crucifix. Herby's evil spirit was a scoffer hidden inside him that could be summoned forth by the genie who lives in liquor bottles.

I first met Herby years ago when we happened to be in the same In Service class at Quantico. Herby was a lowly supervisor at SOG then, but he had recently finished a term as inspector's aide and had reportedly collected enough shrunken credentials to foretell an inevitable rise in the Bureau.

"Stay away from that sneaky bastard," one of the Academy firearms instructors told me privately. "He went through the Detroit office like shit through a tin horn and got a whole bunch of agents busted and transferred."

That statement caused me to be irresistibly drawn to Herby, as the psychiatrist is drawn to the cell of the dangerous mental case or Marlin Perkins to the cage of a puff adder. I arranged to work next to Herby in the butts on the rifle range, jerking and scoring targets. I sat next to him in the dining room, where he hunched over his food like a suspicious dog who is afraid someone will take his plate away from him. In class, when he would occasionally interrupt the lecturer and correct him on some obscure point or other, I would smile at him approvingly and nod in agreement. After two or three days of such overtures he condescended to speak with me in the hall at breaks and even shared some of his problems with me. In his section at SOG he had unscrupulous enemies who were continually working against him. Every morning when we came down to breakfast he would stop off in the SAC's office, ask me to guard the door for him, and then call his rabbi at SOG on the telephone and hold long, whispered conversations while I stood in the hall out of earshot. Apparently his rabbi spent most of his time observing the movements of Herby's enemies. Sometimes the conversations went on for as long as fifteen minutes. Herby's mood for the day depended upon the reports he received from the morning telephone calls. If the news was good, he would sit down to breakfast in good spirits. On those mornings, since he had a weight problem, he would drink black coffee with artificial sweetener and confine his eating to nibbling a piece of unbuttered toast. If the news was bad, he would scurry wordlessly into the dining room, slump into a chair, stare into space, and consume vast portions of eggs, bacon, buttered toast, two or three sweet rolls, and several cups of coffee into which he had dumped teaspoon after teaspoon of sugar.

One night after a bad morning telephone call he and I walked together into the town of Quantico to drink beer at the River View Hotel. You could drink sitting at the bar or buy your beer there and carry it to a table. He pushed past me and ordered a pitcher of beer.

"I'll split it with you or buy the next one," I said.

"Get your own," he said. "This is mine." Then he went to a table carrying his pitcher while I ordered a stein and followed him.

The beer disappeared from his pitcher as fast as the food at breakfast. Somewhere he had learned to inhale beer.

A couple of hours later I stood up to go to the men's room before we left the beer joint to walk back to the Academy. I asked if he wanted to accompany me.

"I'm going to save mine up," he said, "so I can piss on Stone's lawn when we get back to the Academy."

I thought he was kidding. Stone was the SAC at the Academy and very fastidious about the premises.

"He may have the duty tonight," I warned. There was a bedroom adjoining the SAC's office in the Academy, and Stone or one of the firearms instructors had to sleep there every night to make sure the doors were locked at eleven o'clock and that everyone was signed in on the register.

"I hope he does," said Herby. "I'll piss on him if he gets in the way."

We walked down the single main street of Quantico, passed the railroad station, and then turned left to walk under the big trees that lined the street in front of the old red brick Marine barracks. The Academy building was about a mile from the railroad station. Herby was humming to himself, and there was a slight roll to his walk. "I'm just about going to make it," he chuckled. "But don't jar me, boy. Don't jar me. I don't want to let it go too soon."

When we arrived at the Academy building it was still fairly early, and there was no one hanging around outside. Herby stood in the middle of the immaculate lawn in front of the building and unzipped his fly. Then to my horror he started yelling, "Hey, Stone, you redheaded son of a bitch, I'm pissing on your goddam lawn!"

The bright beam of a flashlight lit up Herby like the spotlight on a lone performer on a darkened stage.

"What the hell are you doing, Herby?" It was the firearms instructor who had previously warned me about Herby's raid on Detroit.

"I'm pissing on your lawn, Stone," Herby kept yelling.

"He's got a kidney problem," I said. "He's been on medication and just had one beer . . ."

"Don't give me that bullshit!" the instructor snarled. "He's got a head problem. That's what he's got. If Stone was here and caught him pissing on his lawn like that, both of you would be fired by daylight."

The instructor, as lean and powerful as Herby was pudgy, grabbed Herby's wrist and elbow in a "come along" grip that caused Herby to utter a little shriek of pain and rise on his toes like Rudolf Nureyev doing "Swan Lake." I followed as the instructor made his captive tiptoe into the Academy. I signed us both in on the register while the instructor escorted Herby upstairs in the elevator.

The instructor came back in a few minutes and said, "Go up there and keep that squirrel quiet. If Stone hears about this, we've *all* had it. Herby'll get it for pissing

on the lawn and indecent exposure on a government
reservation. You'll get it for being with him. And I'll get
it for not reporting both of you. I'm going out now
and turn on the sprinklers. I hope idiot urine don't kill
grass."

Upstairs Herby was sitting in his underwear alone in
a room reading *Masters of Deceit* by J. Edgar Hoover.
"C'mere, c'mere," he said. "Gotta read you something
that's very ironic." He peered owlishly down at the
book. "In this very ironic section of his masterpiece my
Director describes the disciplinary procedures of the
Commonist Party. I pernounce it 'commonist' because
that's the way our Leader pernounces it, see? Commonist. The world's full of Commonists. Everybody who
doesn't kiss his ass is a Commonist."

"You better watch out, Herby," I said. "This place
may be bugged. The sewers around here are full of alligators. They may come up out of the commodes and eat
you alive, ambition and all."

"You old Commonist, you," Herby giggled. "I'll piss
on those alligators. You just listen to what our Leader
says about Commonist Party discipline and see if it
reminds you of any other organization." Then, before I
went to bed, he read me the section on Party discipline.

At that time *Masters of Deceit* had been in print for a
year or so, but I had never read it. I later bought a paper-
back and reread the section on Communist Party discipline that Herby read that night. Strangely enough, the
penalties meted out to errant Communist Party members
as described in the Director's book *were* identical to
those given errant FBI agents.

The next morning we had to get up early to board
the Bureau bus back to Washington. Herby did not
appear in the dining room for breakfast. He was already
on the bus when I got on. I sat down next to him. He

was his old fearful and wary self. "Did that firearms instructor report us for last night?" he asked out of the corner of his mouth.

"Us?"

"Dammit, you were as drunk as I was. And I'm taking medication. I've a brother-in-law who's a doctor who will swear I'm taking medication that makes me piss all the time."

"Tell that to Stone," I said.

"Did he report it to Stone? My God, we're done for. I thought he was your friend. Did he really tell Stone?"

"No, I saw him at breakfast. He said he ought to stick it in you for what you did to those guys at Detroit but he figures life is too short to play that game."

Herby breathed a sigh of relief. "Then his ass is in a crack too. If he hasn't reported it by this time, it's too damn late now. They'd stack his ass in the same pile with ours. We've got him where we want him now." He was almost gloating.

"I wish you'd quit saying *us* and *ours* and *we*," I said. "I didn't piss on Stone's grass. You did."

"Yes, but you were there!" Herby whispered out the corner of his mouth. "You were there and you didn't report it. That's just the same as doing it. It's worse in fact. And I don't appreciate the way that jockstrap knucklehead twisted my arm and made that crack about the inspection in Detroit. That's all I seem to hear about any more—Detroit, Detroit, Detroit. I found three subs on the ASAC's desk in Detroit. And he got busted and transferred to Butte. Along with three shaggy-assed agents who had the cases assigned to them. One went to Pittsburgh, one to Oklahoma City, and the other one to Milwaukee. One of them was a big cracker bastard who was about to get an office of preference transfer to Atlanta. He called me on the phone anonymously and said,

'Herby, you ole mothuh fuckuh, if Ah catch you out in an alley, Ah'm gonna kick yo ass so hahd, you'll have to unbutton yo collah to shit.' I thought it was some nigger talking till I figured out who it was. I reported the call to the Inspection Division and the dumb son of a bitch owned up to making the call. They suspended him thirty days. I think I could have got him fired except he's a veteran and the Administrative Division was afraid he'd ask for a hearing. Then his wife had a miscarriage and they put him back on duty because they were afraid he'd file some sort of civil action about that. They should have fired his ass for threatening me like that on the telephone. After all, I was the Director's personal representative while inspecting that office. He told me so before I went to Detroit."

There was Herby the Schizo for you. His rise in the Bureau after that was not meteoric, but it was steady. He made ASAC and survived several inspections in two different offices before going back to SOG for a final tour on the goons. He turned up as head goon to inspect the office where I was assigned, but I don't recall that he perpetrated any unusual atrocities. Just the usual ones. Maybe by then his collection of shrunken credentials was complete. I went to the headquarters city during the inspection and he reluctantly acknowledged our acquaintance with a clammy handshake, although he seemed unable to remember exactly where we had met before. Maybe he really couldn't remember. A lot of dirty tricks had tracked up his brain by then.

Then I heard he had been promoted to SAC of one of the large offices. He finally made it, I thought to myself. The sons of bitches always win. Then the grapevine suddenly crackled with electricity and sent the signal, "Herby the SAC has been shot down. Herby the SAC has been shot down. He insulted the Director and the

Director's missile caught him in midflight, blowing off his ass and genitalia. When he crashed to earth, his ears and eyebrows were burnt off as well."

Well, that was really something. "What did he do? What did he do?" I asked the grapevine. But the grapevine was reticent. When I put in the call letters all I got was a crazy flashing of lights with the message, "Fear, Bullshit, Insecurity, and applause, et cetera, et cetera." All I could learn was that it had been very bad and the Director had wanted to fire Herby for whatever it was but had been restrained by cooler heads in the Administrative Division who reminded him that Herby was a veteran. So all the Director did was bust Herby to the bricks of a doghouse office. The bust cost Herby about $6,000 a year in salary and gave him a big black cloud for a hat. As soon as he made retirement he leaped into the maw of a large corporation. He is probably still in there, knife in hand, cutting his way to the heart of the technostructure.

I heard some of the details of Herby's downfall on the porch of the old Hotel Coronado in sunny Southern California from Jack Lonsdale, who had been a supervisor in the office where Herby was shot down. We were waiting for a bus back to San Diego.

"I had met this guy Herby before, in Washington or somewhere," Lonsdale said, "but I didn't realize he was so goddam strange. Oh, I know, you expect a new SAC to be strange, and you're a little surprised if he isn't, but I never saw one who was strange in the same ways that Herby was. He came to town without his family, and we got him a cut-rate room at the Athletic Club. His wife was still in Memphis or Albany or wherever it was he transferred in from. She was trying to sell the house and get the kids through the school semester. Herby would hang out in the bar of the Athletic Club and bat the breeze with every half-assed character who wandered by. The Director used to visit our field division once in a while, and he had a lot of friends and enemies, or admirers and detractors if you want to call them that, among the prominent people who hung around the Athletic Club. We tried to warn Herby about the pitfalls of talking to some of these people, but you couldn't tell the guy anything. Especially after he had a couple of drinks. After a few weeks in town, he thought he knew everything about everybody. Even after his wife and kids arrived and they got a house, he still spent almost every evening in that bar. Some of the people he talked to were media people. Some were lawyers. Some were the racing crowd that the Director had met at the track. Others were sort of borderline characters in rackets or politics.

"The ASAC came to my office one day all upset and closed the door. His hemorrhoids must have been bothering him, because he tried sitting down, then jumped up and wouldn't stop walking around. 'Jack,' he said to me, 'this new SAC is a nut. I had some drinks with him last night in that Athletic Club bar where he hangs out, and he mouthed off some opinions about the Director you wouldn't believe. If any of his remarks get back to SOG, they'll put out a contract for him and the Stukas will be over this office before sundown. And that's not all. There's a prominent lawyer who hangs out there who's going to be given a big testimonial dinner, and Herby has agreed to be toastmaster or master of ceremonies or something. I told him that lawyer was *persona non grata* with the Director. You know what he said? 'Screw the Director,' he said. Just sort of yelled it out in that goddam bar. You know the unwritten rule. You're supposed to lose control and knock anybody who says anything

like that about the Director on his ass. But I was so surprised I just sat there with my mouth open. And then
Herby says to me, 'Screw you too.' He said he'd been
going through the cases on my desk and found a couple
of pretty good subs, and if I gave him any static he'd
have my ass. We've got to call the Bureau and report
this to protect ourselves.' "

Lonsdale shook his head ruefully at the memory.
" 'Whoa, boy,' I told the ASAC. 'Let's forget that *we*
stuff. I'm just sitting here supervising these applicant
cases, trying to survive. I'm not about to call the Bureau
and make a report on the SAC. I don't hang out in that
bar so I don't know what goes on there. I just do my
work here and go home at night to my wife and family
and watch television and think pure thoughts. Squirrelly
SACs are nothing new to me. I've worked under at least
a dozen. When this one goes, they'll send us another,
maybe worse. They've got a whole cage full of them up
there at SOG. Get rid of one and you get another one.
Forget that call to the Bureau. If we complain about the
SAC, the inspectors will come down and try to knock *us*
off, not him.' "

According to Lonsdale, what finally took Herby out
was the testimonial dinner. He rented formal evening
attire and made his appearance at the head table. A large
crowd of people attended, including many of the habi-
tués of the Athletic Club bar. At some stage of the fes-
tivities Herby was at the microphone trading badinage
with other guests. One of them said something like,
"You're a big man in charge of the FBI in this area,
Herby. Can you do everything the Director can do?"

"Well, of course," said Herby with a suggestive leer,
"being a comparatively young man, I can still do some
things he can no longer do."

(*Background laughter and riotous applause.*)

"However, he can still do one thing I can't do," Herby said.

"What's that, Herby?" All of his beautiful friends were anxious to hear.

"Walk on water," said Herby. "I haven't learned to walk on water the way he can yet."

(*Whee! More background laughter and riotous applause. Flashbulbs popping and the bright television lights like magnesium flares and all the beautiful laughing people and Herby standing there in his rented formal attire like Jackie Gleason killing them in Vegas. Herby, the center of attraction of all those wonderful, beautiful, laughing people.*)

Unknown to Herby there were alligators in the sewers of that city. One of them popped up in the crowd and peeked out to observe the proceedings at the party. This particular alligator was a news columnist who was a great admirer of the Director. He had his tape recorder with him and recorded Herby's disrespectful remarks about the Director's supernatural powers. These remarks irritated the newsman exceedingly. He was a believer in, and a perpetuator of, the myth.

Next morning there were pictures of the party in the newspapers, and prominently photographed was Herby, the life of the party himself, standing between the guest of honor and an attractively dressed female of mature years but comely appearance. Herby had his arm around her waist. The picture fanned the irritation of the newsman to fury. The personal representative of his idol, Mr. Hoover, had his arm around the waist of one of the most notorious madams on the West Coast.

Quivering with indignation, the newsman dispatched a copy of the photograph and a copy of his tape to the Director. They exploded like bombs in the slumbering volcano at the height of SOG. A fountain of molten lava gushed forth, landing with a resounding splat on Herby's head.

"It was kind of awful but funny too, in a horrible sort of way," Lonsdale said. "The chief inspector worked Herby over all morning in his office, probably ramming an umbrella up his ass and opening it several times. He must have gotten some sort of statement from Herby. Then he called a closed meeting of all supervisors that afternoon. He brought Herby in and made him apologize personally to all the supervisors for embarrassing the Bureau, for embarrassing the office, for embarrassing the Director, for embarrassing the whole damn universe. Herby looked smaller. You know, like a balloon with just enough air let out of it to be sort of baggy. He started crying before it was over. My God, we *were* embarrassed then. Oh, occasionally somebody he had shafted would snicker, and that would set off the chief inspector into a tirade. Then the powers did something I thought was damned Russian. They busted Herby and shipped him out on the bricks, and on probation, to Omaha or Buffalo or somewhere, and he had to be out of town by five o'clock that afternoon! He couldn't even go home and kiss his wife goodby. He called her on the phone and told her where to send a suitcase, and the inspector took him out to the airport and put him on the next plane to the doghouse. There was something damned Russian about it, I'll tell you that."

"Well, I guess Herby knew what he was talking about when he said the Old Man got his ideas about Bureau discipline from the Commonist Party," I said. "Herby got everything but expulsion, the final blow for Party members."

"He'd have got that too," said Lonsdale, "except he was a veteran. That's the only thing that saved him."

12

The Director Descends from Olympus

In the fall of 1959 the Director must have been pawing through the seeds of time—as the Bard has phrased it—trying to decide which grains would grow and which would not. The seeds were Presidential aspirants. As a result of the pawing, he decided that destiny called him to Texas for a visit. The particular Lone Star seed which excited his interest was Lyndon B. Johnson. So it turned out that J. Edgar Hoover and his associate director, Clyde Tolson, appeared on the blasted heath of Texas that fall to examine this exciting seed at close range.

The offstage signal that presaged their appearance was not a foreboding drum but a ring of the telephone in the office of the Fort Worth Resident Agency, where I was assigned, one bright morning in early November. It was the SAC in Dallas calling. He spoke at some length with Tom Carter, the senior resident agent. During the conversation Carter's good-humored expression gradually became glum. When he had hung up, Carter said, "The SAC wants me in Dallas this morning. The Director

plans to come to Texas next week to visit Lyndon Johnson in Austin. I'm supposed to help out."

"Austin is in the San Antonio division," I said.

"There are no direct nonstop flights from Washington
to Austin," said Carter. "The Director will fly to Dallas,
and I have to drive him to Austin in a car."

"Will it be bad?" I asked.

"It can't be good," Carter said. "I was assigned to the
Oklahoma City office in 1938 when he came down to
accept an honorary degree from Oklahoma Baptist University at Shawnee. It wasn't much fun. He and Mr.
Tolson can really keep everyone on edge."

"Will Tolson be here too?"

"Oh, yes," said Carter. "Wherever the Director goes,
Mr. Tolson goes too."

Clyde Anderson Tolson, Associate Director of the
FBI, was the Director's closest friend. He had the reputation of being the super hatchet man in the FBI, an
agency swarming with hatchet men.

"Well," said Carter, "if you just look at the whole
thing as a sort of nutty vaudeville show, maybe you can
keep your sense of humor and make it to retirement
without developing an ulcer." At that time Carter had a
year's service remaining to qualify for retirement. "If
they sent me to Anchorage or Timbuktu, I would have
to go. I've got too much time invested in the Bureau
not to."

In 1959 I had been a special agent for ten years and
had never experienced a visit from the Director. Although the prospect was frightening, it was also fascinat-
ing. At last I might have the opportunity to observe the
Director on my own turf, far from his center of power,
the throne room office in the Justice Building, above the
corner of Pennsylvania Avenue and Ninth Street in
Washington, D.C.

By 1959 the days of the violent 1930s, when he had personally led raids into the Field to arrest such public rats as Alvin "Creepy" Karpis in New Orleans and Louis "Lepke" Buchalter in New York, were all in the distant past. His legend was secure. He no longer had to prove he was the nation's leading crime fighter.

By 1959 there were only a few offices of the Field that he and Mr. Tolson visited regularly. Every August they spent two or three weeks in the San Diego area at La Jolla, in a bungalow at the Hotel del Charro, as guests of the hotel owner, a Dallas oil man named Clint Murchison. During the mornings Mr. Hoover went through his annual physical checkup at the Scripps Clinic, and in the afternoons he generally went to the Del Mar racetrack. They went to New York every New Year's to celebrate the Director's birthday, and later in January they visited Miami Beach, occupying a beach house at the Gulf Stream Hotel owned by the Schine family. Occasionally they went to Los Angeles and San Francisco, renewing acquaintanceships with such old friends as Shirley Temple and Dorothy Lamour.

I had long before chosen the Field as my home and looked upon SOG as enemy territory. The Field was pleasant if you were a fox and not an eagle. The only really bad times came during the annual office inspections. Then the foxes had to scatter and impersonate rabbits in order not to become "it" in the most dangerous game.

Despite my antipathy toward SOG, I had, like most agents, a deep curiosity about the Director. I longed to study him up close, to observe for myself his visage and his actions and try to figure out what was really behind that cloud of mystique. After all, if he was really a living lion, anything he said or did merited the interest of a fox.

On that bright day in 1959 when Carter received the

telephone call, I developed business at headquarters myself. I decided to go with him to Dallas and review my case files. This was fine with Carter; he enjoyed company. I packed my own briefcase and rode with him in his 1959 Ford sedan. We showed our FBI credentials to the man in one of the booths at the toll plaza of the Dallas–Fort Worth Turnpike, and he handed us a free ticket. Then we split the wind the thirty miles to Dallas.

Leaving the car in the contract parking garage, we walked the few blocks to the Federal Building at 1114 Commerce, where the FBI field office was then housed. The weather was sunny but cold, welcome after the heat of the long Texas summer. People on the street were smiling and cheerful. As we walked, a Boeing 707 jet airliner flew low over the building tops, circling to land at Love Field. The huge aircraft made a whistling rumble, causing the canyons between the buildings to vibrate with sound. Since commercial jets were still a novelty in 1959, Carter and I stopped and craned our necks upward to watch it.

"I'm going to ride one of those my next trip to SOG," I said. All agents had to attend two-week In-Service training sessions in Washington every two years, and I was almost due to go.

"I'll still take the train," said Carter. "I'm never in a hurry to get to SOG."

Carter and I both liked to ride the train. We liked to eat in the dining car, to sleep in roomettes at night, and during the day, as the train rumbled along, to look out the window at the farms and small towns and wonder what people were doing out there. I was never in a hurry to get to SOG myself, but I resolved to ride the jet next time.

When we reached the field office we signed our names on the register to record our time of arrival, and Carter hurried off to see the SAC. I went into the chief clerk's office and collected a yard-high stack of files on which I intended to dictate memoranda, letters, and reports. I found a vacant desk and had just settled down to work when I heard my name called over the public address system. I picked up a telephone and the operator connected me with Carter. "Come to the boss's office," he said. "You have to help out on this one too." I closed the file I was looking at, straightened my necktie, and ran a comb through my hair. I had a sense of anticipation that I was about to become involved in something really significant.

Looking back on it now, I can think of three reasons why the Dallas SAC picked me as one of the agents to help out with the Director's visit. I was thin; I was assigned to my office of preference, and I did not smoke. As I have said, being thin was very important to the Director.

Being assigned to my office of preference was important, because it made me more trustworthy. I would be very careful around the Director not to screw up and risk a disciplinary transfer.

My being a nonsmoker was extremely important to the SAC personally, because he was a health nut. He abhorred tobacco smoke. After the departure of any visitor who had smoked in his office, the SAC would spray out the room with a deodorant and open his windows, even on the coldest day, and stand in front of the windows a long time, taking deep breaths.

The SAC kept himself in excellent physical condition with daily calisthenics and bicycle riding. He had been captain of his college tumbling team and during his early Bureau career had acted as the "fall guy" in judo exhibitions at the FBI Academy, because his training as a tumbler had taught him to fall without getting hurt. This had been back in the 1940s, when judo was a big thing in the Bureau. He was very proud of his ability to walk on his hands—another holdover from college tumbling days—and would demonstrate this skill without much urging. I can see him now, clad in a conservative business suit, walking around his office on his hands, keys, change, and other odds and ends from his pockets rattling to the floor and his necktie dragging along below his upended chin, under the astonished gaze of some visitor he was trying to impress.

The SAC occupied a large corner office with brown paneled walls and shuttered windows. The decorations were standard FBI: an American flag drooping from a pole in one corner, an autographed photograph of J. Edgar Hoover frowning from the wall behind the desk, and a photograph of the current President—Dwight D. Eisenhower—staring benignly from another wall. At the end of President Eisenhower's term his picture would be replaced immediately with that of the new President. Only the flag and Mr. Hoover's picture were eternal.

When I entered the SAC's office that morning, Carter and several other agents were there, seated in chairs and on a long leather couch against one wall. They were all listening to the SAC, who did not stop talking when I came in. I closed the door behind me quietly and sat down on the couch between Jack Bain and Sid Bowser, two agents assigned to the headquarters city.

The SAC was addressing the group on one of his favorite themes, a theory of office management he called the "halo effect." This theory held that the secret of running a successful FBI office was the creation of such an overpoweringly favorable first impression on any visiting official from SOG that it would blind him to any defects that might crop up later during the course of the visit.

The halo effect had been on the SAC's mind often during the past weeks. We knew this very well because the SAC was a man who did not keep his problems to himself. He shared them with the people around him. Practically everything that entered his mind almost immediately jumped out his mouth, especially when he was nervous. And he had good reason to be nervous these days. Dallas was overdue for its annual office inspection, and the SAC had received a telephone call from a friend at SOG passing the word that one of the assistant directors was out to shoot him down over Dallas. The SAC never said why this assistant director disliked him. Perhaps he did not know why. The assistant director may have observed the SAC walking on his hands and thought it undignified. He may have been jealous of the SAC's physique, which was so trim most of the other officials appeared fat and clumsy in comparison. Or the assistant director may have been the rabbi of someone who yearned to be king of Dallas, the way Arthur had yearned to be king of Knoxville. Whatever the reason, the grapevine said there was a contract out for the SAC, and the next office inspection was going to be a ballbuster.

As I took my seat on the couch, the SAC was bringing his halo effect theory to bear on the Director's visit.

"Although I have had no indication whatsoever that he might actually visit this office," the SAC was saying, "I cannot assume that he will not. I have put everyone on the alert that he may. All desks, filing cabinets, floors, and walls must be scrubbed and spotless. All male personnel must wear white shirts and subdued neckties. I am seriously considering making all fat employees take annual leave and hide out at home."

I took a pencil from my jacket pocket and doodled on a pad of paper, because I knew the SAC liked to see that. He always said it made for good halo effect to take notes of everything a superior Bureau official said to you.

"Another point which I think is important," he said, "is what *not* to say, if any of you have occasion to engage in personal conversation with the Director or Mr. Tolson." He looked at us grimly. "I would suggest you limit your conversation with them to 'yes, sir' and 'no, sir.' At no time infer they are down here on vacation or to have a good time. Remember, they *never* take vacations. They are on official business for the Bureau twenty-four hours a day, seven days a week. Never forget that. Don't volunteer any ass-kissing remarks to either of them, and don't ask for any o.p. transfers. It might be fatal."

The SAC looked down at a note pad covered with scribbling. "I've been on the phone several times this morning with Nick Callahan, and he's filled me in on some important points we have to cover."

Nick Callahan was an assistant director at SOG. Apparently he was handling the details of Mr. Hoover's trip.

"I'll fill you guys in," said the SAC. "There will probably be additional instructions coming in all week."

For the next half-hour the SAC filled us in. As he had said, there were some important points to cover.

The Director and Mr. Tolson would arrive November 8 at Love Field, Dallas, early in the afternoon on American Airlines and would immediately depart by car for Austin, where they would spend the night in the Stephen F. Austin Hotel. On the following morning they would be greeted by Senator Lyndon Johnson. At noon the Director would make the principal address at the state reporting luncheon of the United Fund.

After the luncheon the Director and Mr. Tolson would say goodby to Senator Lyndon Johnson and return to Dallas by car. They would spend Monday night at the Sheraton Hotel in Dallas and return to Washington next morning on American Airlines.

Tom Carter was to drive them in a Cadillac limousine to Austin and back. I was to follow at a discreet distance in a Bureau car to be available in case of emergency. The SAC at Dallas and the SAC at San Antonio (in whose field division Austin was located) had been informed by Callahan that their presence was unnecessary in Austin. This meant that they were not to appear unless summoned. Carter and I and the Austin resident agents would be responsible for the welfare of the Director and Mr. Tolson while they were in Austin.

The plan sounded simple, but it was not. Callahan had relayed a multitude of instructions that would complicate even the simplest procedures. For example, the baggage of the Director and Mr. Tolson could be handled only by special agents and had to be the last baggage placed aboard any departing aircraft and the first baggage taken off after the plane landed.

"The Director and Mr. Tolson will not tolerate delay over baggage," said the SAC. "Bain, you will make arrangements with the airline on how to handle this. Bob Green and another agent will be responsible for getting the bags from the luggage compartment of the plane to the trunk of the Cadillac, immediately after the plane lands."

"O.K.," said Bain, "but we'll have to know exactly how many bags they have and exactly what they look like in order to get the right ones off. We can't afford to get the wrong luggage."

"Right," said the SAC, making a note. "I'll ask Callahan. Now, Jack, make arrangements with American Airlines to park the Cadillac on the landing area, close to the terminal building, just outside their VIP room."

The VIP room was a private room in the terminal with

its own entrance to the landing area, a room furnished with leather chairs and couches where celebrities could be greeted and interviewed by the press undisturbed by the rabble in the public waiting rooms.

"Oh," said Bain, a thought striking him on hearing the SAC mention the VIP room. "Is the press going to be notified about this visit?"

"Absolutely not," said the SAC. "Callahan was very specific on that. No press release on Dallas arrival or departure. Make that clear to American Airlines public relations, Jack. The Director doesn't like all that pushing and shoving and being asked questions when he gets on or off an airplane."

"O.K.," said Bain, "but if some reporter happens to be hanging around there and spots him . . ."

"Jack, you know most of the press people around here on sight, don't you?"

"Well," said Bain warily, suspecting a trap, "I guess I know a lot of them."

"O.K.," said the SAC, "if you see any of them hanging around the American Airlines VIP room about the time the Director's plane arrives, just sidle up and say, 'I just heard a rumor that the Governor and his wife are in the Braniff VIP room waiting for a flight to Buenos Aires or Rio de Janeiro.' They'll get all excited wondering why the Governor is going to South America and run off to find out. Braniff is way off at the other end of the terminal. By the time they get back, we'll be gone."

"A trick like that would really screw up future press relations," said Bain.

The SAC smiled. "Jack, if we allow a press reporter to annoy the Old Man when he gets off that plane, *we* won't have any future press relations here in Dallas. Understand?"

"Yes, Boss," said Bain.

The SAC continued: "After Bob Green gets the luggage into the trunk and I get the Director and Mr. Tolson inside the car, Carter will drive the Cadillac to Austin along a prescribed route." The SAC looked at me. "Joe, you will follow in a Bureau car, but for God's sake don't be too obvious. Hang back . . . but not too far back. Try to be inconspicuous. But if anything does happen to the Cadillac on the road, God forbid, like a drunk running into it or a flat tire or something, you swoop down, scoop up the Director and Mr. Tolson, bag and baggage, and blast off for Austin. They won't tolerate any delay. But here's another thing that Callahan mentioned. Don't own up to having followed them on purpose. They don't like that. Just say something like, 'I just happened by, et cetera, et cetera, and recognized you, and am available to take you wherever you're going.' Play it dumb, see."

"Do you think they'd believe that?" I asked. "We're out on the highway somewhere and I just happen by and happen to recognize them?"

"Don't argue," said the SAC. "Don't argue over trifles and nitpick. Just do as I say. O.K.?"

"Sure, Boss," I said. "I'll say anything you want me to say. But if I were the Director or Mr. Tolson, I wouldn't believe a story like that. If I were the Director or Mr. Tolson, I would—"

"Joe," said the SAC, "You have delusions of grandeur. You are not the Director and you are not Mr. Tolson. You are a shaggy-assed resident agent on the bricks in Fort Worth. So will you please stop arguing so that we can get on with this?"

"Sure, Boss," I said, "but I still can't understand—"

"Shut up," said the SAC.

"Yes, sir."

"Just keep in mind," the SAC said in a conciliatory tone, "that if something *does* happen to the Cadillac,

and you *do* have to take them over for the trip to Austin,
the only thing that will save us all is the line of bullshit
you lay on them after you pick them up. Our careers, so
to speak, will be in your hands. Is that clear?"

"Yes," I said. My feeling of excitement began to wane
and a sense of foreboding replaced it. I began to wish I
had stayed home in Fort Worth and attended to my investigative chores. If something happened to the Cadillac
and I had to drive the Director and Mr. Tolson to Austin, I might very well become the victim of one of their
instant and irrevocable decisions. If I made a poor impression, I could be transferred from my desirable resident agency assignment to snowswept exile in an Alaskan
igloo. On the other hand, if I made too good an impression, I might be promoted to SOG, a fate as gloomy to
contemplate as the icy clime of Anchorage. How would
I ever explain such a transfer to my wife? What about
my new car, not yet paid for? What about my house
mortgage? I resolved to tread carefully. If I did come
under the personal scrutiny of the Director and Mr. Tolson, I would be careful to exhibit a competency sufficient
only for my present assignment, no more, no less.

"The route to Austin presents problems," said the
SAC.

That broke my reverie. To drive from Dallas to Austin, all you had to do was head south about two hundred
miles on a broad interstate highway that was divided into
four lanes most of the way.

"There's no sweat about that, Boss," I said. "We just
get on 77 and aim south—"

"There's one catch," said the SAC. "There will be no
left turns."

That startled everybody. But, of course, there was a
good explanation. In California several months before,
the Director's chauffeur-driven car, while making a left

turn, had been struck by another car from behind. The Director had been shaken up. He had been sitting on the left side behind the driver. Now he refused to sit on the left rear seat any more and had forbidden all left turns on auto trips.

"He makes Mr. Tolson sit behind the driver now," said the SAC. "According to Callahan, the Director calls that side the 'death seat.' "

"They could both sit on the right side," said Carter, "if one would sit in the other's lap."

The SAC frowned at Carter. "This is nothing to joke about, Tom. You know how dead serious anything to do with the Director or Mr. Tolson can be."

"Just kidding, Boss," Carter said.

Looking at Sid Bowser, the SAC said, "Sid, you are responsible for the hotel accommodations at the Sheraton for Monday night. Do you have your instructions straight?"

Sid consulted some notes on a sheet of paper. "Need suite consisting of living room and two bedrooms. Each bedroom must have private bath. Each bedroom must have double bed. Mattresses must be not too hard, not too soft, must be just right. Four pillows on each bed—"

"Down pillows!" said the SAC. "Down pillows on each bed!"

"O.K., O.K.," said Sid, making a note. "Four down pillows on each bed. All appliances in rooms, such as radios and television sets, must have typed instructions explaining how to turn on and turn off. Typing must be neat. Check closely for misspelling and typographical errors. Decorative flowers may be placed in suite living room but not in bedrooms. Basket full of fruit may be placed on coffee table of living room. If liquor placed in suite, Director drinks Jack Daniels and Mr. Tol—"

"Jack Daniels *black label*, Sid!" said the SAC. "Let's get that right!"

"O.K., O.K." Sid made another note.

"You see?" The SAC looked around at us with an I-told-you-so expression. "You see why we have to plan and plan and plan these things? One little slip and Mr. Tolson will eat up this office like I used to eat Cracker Jacks when I was a kid."

"O.K.," said Bowser, "Mr. Tolson drinks Grant's Scotch, the eight-year-old, not the twelve-year-old, right?"

"Right," said the SAC, "be sure and check the bottle labels. Now, Sid, in regard to that suite and the hotel arrangements, you are responsible. Understand? *You are responsible.* Don't depend on the hotel manager or the housekeeper or the maid to make sure that suite is ship-shape prior to their arrival. Do it yourself. Check the suite completely. Make sure the beds are made up neatly and that the bathrooms are spotless and that all the towels and soap, et cetera, et cetera, are there. Make sure the drapes work smoothly when you pull the little rope. Sometimes they get stuck." A thoughtful expression crossed his face. "Maybe I should get my wife to check out the place before they arrive. She can find more things wrong with a hotel room than Conrad Hilton." Then he shook his head. "No, no, better not, better not. She might drop a bobby pin somewhere and they might think we were turning the place into a whorehouse. You'll have to handle it, Sid. Be sure and flush the toilets. Make sure they flush downward and not upward. In Miami once the toilet in the Director's bathroom went up like a geyser when he flushed it. Mr. Tolson put the SAC and the ASAC both on probation. And ashtrays, for God's sake make sure all ashtrays are clean. The Director doesn't smoke any more, but Mr. Tolson does and both are finicky as hell about neatness. Neither of them will tolerate dirty ashtrays. Look under the beds. Check all bureau drawers. It would be just my luck for Mr. Tolson to find a dead rat in one of the drawers. We'd never survive it. Also, check with the hotel manager to make sure a house doctor is available in case one of them gets sick. Find out who the doctor is. Check him out and make sure he looks and acts O.K. If there is an emergency and they need a doctor—" the SAC held up one finger "—number one, I want to be sure a doctor is available fast, and number two—" he held up a second finger "—I want to be sure the doctor looks and acts O.K., not like a fairy or a hophead or a pharmacist's mate off a Chinese gunboat."

"Tell you what, Boss," said one of the Dallas agents, "My bridge club meets Monday night and my own doctor is a member. I might get him to sort of stand by, you know, be available. If the Director or Mr. Tolson did get sick, I could run him over to the hotel in nothing flat. My doctor used to play pro football. He looks and acts O.K."

The SAC gazed at the agent thoughtfully. "That sounds like a good idea, but keep in mind that if something does happen, I need to be called at once. I would need to be on the scene too."

The SAC was not going to allow one of his subordinates to run to the aid of the Director or Mr. Tolson with a doctor at a time of physical crisis and exclude him. Later, Mr. Tolson might murmur reflectively, "Eddie, I wonder where the agent in charge was last night when you had the acute indigestion" or "that sudden pain." And that would be the end of the SAC.

Improving on his first idea, the agent said, "We might even have the doctor call up Mr. Hoover during the course of the evening and say something like, 'I've always been a great admirer of yours and wonder if you feel all right?' "

The SAC shook his head. "No, no, that's absolutely the wrong way to pitch it. Nick Callahan said no publicity. If some doctor calls up out of the blue asking the Old Man about his health, that might get us all blown out. Just keep the doctor on the alert." He turned to Bowser. "Go by the Chamber of Commerce and pick up all the brochures they have of general interest about Dallas and this vicinity—industries, history, that kind of stuff. Make up two envelopes of the material, one for each bedroom of the suite. Be damn sure you have exactly the same brochures in each package. I repeat. Be damn sure you have exactly the same stuff in each package. Callahan says that if one gets something the other one doesn't, there's hell to pay."

"I'll check each package," Bowser said.

"Now, about the Cadillac, Jack," said the SAC. "Fill us in on that."

Bain had arranged to borrow a new 1960 model Cadillac from a Dallas car dealer. He would pick up the car several days before the Director's arrival. Carter wanted to practice driving it. "I'm not used to driving a Cadillac," he said, "and I can't afford any drastic mechanical surprises on this trip, like a windshield wiper that won't work."

"Now, Jack," said the SAC, "make sure you get exactly the right kind of car. According to instructions it has to be a black four-door sedan. Don't come back with a yellow convertible, for God's sake! Inside, there must be two black umbrellas and two envelopes containing exactly the road maps and brochures relating to the area through which the trip will be made. The same stuff in each package. This Cadillac must be meticulously clean. Especially inside. Dirty upholstery or dirty ash-trays will not be tolerated. Callahan suggested that the agent chauffeur carry a dust cloth in the glove compartment and on occasions when the Director and Mr. Tolson leave the car for any periods of time, the agent should occupy himself with dusting the car's interior.

"Also, according to Callahan," the SAC continued, "the driver of the Cadillac must not, under any circumstances, exceed the legal speed limits. Mr. Tolson is very particular about this. Callahan said that occasionally Mr. Tolson would lean forward and look over the driver's shoulder at the speedometer. He will not tolerate excessive speed." The SAC looked around at everyone. "That's about all the revelations for today. Any questions?"

There were no questions, but before the meeting broke up the SAC decided that the first logical move was to make a dry run from Love Field, Dallas, to the Stephen F. Austin Hotel in Austin to find out exactly how long the trip would take when all legal speed limits and stop signs were meticulously heeded and all foreseeable causes of delay, such as highway construction and detours, were taken into account. Of course, the most important purpose of the dry run was to eliminate left turns.

As the rest of us left the SAC's office, Carter lagged behind to discuss with the SAC a private matter, which he felt should be resolved before the SAC sent his name up to SOG as the driver of the Cadillac. During the late 1930s Carter had inadvertently made too good an impression on a high-ranking official during an office inspection and had paid for this blunder by being elevated to the heights of SOG—as a supervisor in Mr. Tolson's office. The rarefied air of SOG had had an adverse effect on Carter's health. Working in Mr. Tolson's front office had made his head, his gut, and his rear end throb in melancholy unison. He had consulted a doctor. On learning where he worked, the doctor had told Carter he had treated numerous Bureau supervisors over the years. "You have nothing to look forward to down there but the three H's—hemorrhoids, hypertension, and heart attack," he said with a grim smile. "Everybody down there except Hoover and Tolson has them. My prescription? Go back to Texas where you came from and forget this FBI rat race."

That sounded like good medicine to Carter, but the Depression was in full swing and jobs paying $3,800 a year were hard to find. Any job was hard to find. In Texas lawyers were sleeping on courthouse lawns on summer nights hoping for a chance to bail out arrested prostitutes. Prostitutes were about the only people who had anything to sell that anyone wanted to buy, and selling it was illegal.

Several days later Mr. Tolson, in a seemingly congenial mood, had asked, "What is your ambition in the Bureau, Carter?"

This was an opportunity, Carter decided. "My ambition, Mr. Tolson, is to transfer out of Washington and go back to the Field."

An hour later Carter received a telephone call from the Chief Clerk. "What in the hell did you say to Tolson? He's really given you the business."

Carter told him about the conversation.

"You're going back to the Field, all right," said the Chief Clerk. "Resident agent at Harlan, Kentucky. Bloody Harlan! How about that?"

Carter survived two years in Bloody Harlan, the scene of violent hostilities between coal miners and mine operators, before he finally wangled a transfer home to Dallas. Harlan was twenty years in the past, ancient history to Carter, but he knew that Mr. Tolson had a long memory.

He might still hold a grudge. Carter wanted the SAC to call Nick Callahan and have him ask Mr. Tolson directly if it was all right for him to drive the Cadillac to Austin. "I don't want to surprise him," Carter had confided in me during the trip to Dallas that morning. "I'm too old to go back to Harlan."

A short time later Carter appeared in the agents' room where I was still looking at files. He was smiling. The SAC had called Callahan and Callahan had checked with Tolson. Mr. Tolson had said it was quite agreeable with him for Carter to drive the Cadillac. In fact, Mr. Tolson said, he looked forward with pleasure to seeing Carter again. Apparently time had reconciled him to Carter's lack of ambition. "I guess the statute of limitations has run out on that crime," said Carter.

"Maybe Mr. Tolson is getting mellow in his old age," I said.

"Ho, ho, ho," said Carter.

Next day Carter returned to Dallas, picked up the SAC and another agent, and made the dry run to Austin and back. I was not able to go. At the last minute I was subpoenaed to testify in a trial in the United States District Court in Fort Worth. I knew the way to Austin blindfolded anyway, having attended college there for five years and driven back and forth countless times. When I talked with Carter in Fort Worth on his return, he had good news and bad. The bad news was that there seemed no way to eliminate one left turn leaving Dallas and one left turn leaving Austin on the return trip.

"We'll park on the field by the American Airlines gate where the plane will disembark passengers," he said. "After we get the Old Man and Tolson in the Cad, I'll leave through the main entrance and turn right on Mockingbird Lane. I drive due west until I come to the intersection of Highway 77 to Waco where I *have* to turn south, which means left. But it's a protected turn. There's a traffic light there with a left-turn arrow. The SAC thinks it will be all right but he's going to clear it with Callahan. We go south on Highway 77 to Waco where we go around the traffic circle and take off on Highway 81 to Austin. We drove each way yesterday in slightly less than four hours, observing all the speed limits and stop lights. We checked the rest rooms in several service stations in case they get the urge to go to the john on the way. We found only one that the SAC thought was O.K. That's in a Gulf station on the traffic circle at Waco. He's going to call the resident agent at Waco to make sure it's clean next Sunday afternoon.

"Leaving Austin on our way back," Carter said, "we will have to make a left turn to get back on the freeway north. But it's protected with a stop light too."

Carter reported that the resident agents at Austin had managed to reserve the best suite in the Stephen F. Austin Hotel for the Director and Mr. Tolson, but not without encountering additional problems. On the day before the Director was to arrive, the University of Texas football team was to play Baylor University at Austin. The town would be crowded the entire weekend. To ensure occupancy of the suite for Sunday night, the Austin RA had to rent it for Friday, Saturday *and* Sunday nights at $35 a night. Also, the suite lacked the right kind of furniture: one bedroom had twin beds instead of a double. The SAC had tested all the beds by lying down on them and had pronounced the mattresses too soggy. "Looks like they'll have to rent new furniture for one bedroom and change the mattresses," said Carter. "The RAs keep wondering who's going to pay the extra expenses—the extra two nights and the furniture rental."

"What did the SAC say about that?"

"He said that the Stephen F. Austin Hotel is located in the San Antonio field division," said Carter. "Any problems arising in that division have to be resolved by the SAC at San Antonio."

Carter brought back from Austin the rumor that Lyndon Johnson's main reason for inviting the Director to Austin was to help him win Negro votes. This sounds outlandish today, in the light of Mr. Hoover's later well-publicized differences with Martin Luther King, Jr., but in 1959 J. Edgar Hoover was a living legend to whites and blacks both.

It was common knowledge in 1959 that Johnson intended to seek the Democratic nomination for President in 1960. It was also common knowledge within the Bureau that J. Edgar Hoover favored Vice President Richard M. Nixon to succeed President Eisenhower. He had had a long relationship with Nixon dating back to the Alger Hiss case in the late 1940s and often attended baseball games with Nixon after he became Vice President. The Director once told reporter Ralph de Toledano, "Nixon was a good man to have along. He knew all the players by name and everything about them—batting, fielding, everything." However, realist that he was, Hoover could not overlook the possibility that Johnson *might* get the nomination and *might* get elected. And unquestionably Johnson and Hoover were personal friends, neighbors in fact, having lived across the street from each other for several years on 30th Place in the Northwest Section of Washington.

A day or so later the SAC held another conference in his office. "Callahan called again and gave me a few more items," he said. As usual, the pad on his desk was covered with scribbling. "Take this down, Jack, because it relates to the Cadillac. There have to be two notebooks in the

back seat of the car, one on each armrest, and a well-
sharpened pencil with each."

"What are they going to do? Write notes to each
other?" asked Bowser.

"Cut it, Sid," said the SAC. He was beginning to be
snappish. "Anybody have any idea what the weather
forecast is for Sunday?"

Nobody had heard.

The SAC assumed his I-have-to-think-of-everything-
myself look. "If it's cold, we have to have a lap robe in
the car," he said.

"My God," said Bowser, "I haven't ever heard of anybody using a lap robe in a car in Texas."

The SAC stared at him. "You may hear of a lot of new
things before this is over, Sid."

One of the agents said, "I can probably handle that
if the need arises, Boss. My wife has a lap robe she
bought when we were assigned to Minneapolis in 1945.
It's in a closet somewhere. She never throws anything
away. We had one of those wartime jalopies without a
heater and—"

The SAC interrupted him. "Is your robe dark brown
on one side and white or cream-colored on the other?"

"No, the way I remember it, ours is a dark red with—"

"Then it won't do," said the SAC. "It just won't do.
Callahan says the robe has to be dark brown on one side
and white or cream-colored on the other. It has to be
folded neatly with the dark side out."

"Let's pray for warm weather," said Bowser. "Even
if we found the right color, we might fold it wrong."

"Let's depend on the car heater if the weather gets
chilly," said Carter. "That Cadillac's heater could probably bake him like a cupcake if he gets cold."

"O.K., O.K.," said the SAC, "I'll check with Callahan.
Sid, here's another project for at the hotel."

Bowser picked up his pencil. "What's the latest?"

"Ice cubes," said the SAC. "The Director is very particular about ice cubes. He hates little skimpy ones that melt too fast. He likes big, fat, tough ice cubes that melt very slowly."

Bowser made a note. "I'll talk to the hotel people. Maybe they can freeze him some extra cold, extra big ones."

The SAC studied his list. "Let's see . . . lap robe, ice cubes . . . elevators. Elevators. This is important. The Director and Mr. Tolson will not wait for elevators. Elevators must wait for them. We have to have an elevator ready and waiting for them every time they enter a hotel lobby or leave their suite. When they walk up to the elevator, the car has to be there with the door open or the door has to fly open, boom, so that they can enter without missing a step."

"Jesus Christ!" said Bowser. "At rush hours the elevator lobby in the Sheraton looks like dinner time in a monkey house. The hall is crowded with people pushing to get on and off elevators. If we try to reserve an elevator for just two guys during a rush, we may have a riot."

"These are not just two guys," said the SAC. "These are the Director and Mr. Tolson. An elevator will be reserved. You arrange it, understand?"

"O.K., O.K.," said Bowser.

The SAC said, "Here's an item from right out of left field, and I don't know what brought it up, but if anyone asks you how tall Mr. Hoover is, the authorized answer is 'slightly under six feet.' Get it? 'Slightly under six feet.' That's a sort of sensitive point, I gather."

Everyone wrote that down.

"How tall is he, anyway? Really, I mean?" I asked.

"I think he's a dwarf and everything around him has

to be built to scale to keep him from finding out," one of the baggage-handlers-to-be said.

Several of us laughed.

The SAC cleared his throat and straightened the handsome pen and pencil set on his desk which had been presented to him by the employees of the Salt Lake City office when he had been promoted from a lowly field office supervisor to a position as inspector on the goons and thus began his ascent in the Bureau. "I don't like being a horse's ass about this," he said, "but it seems to me that some of you are not taking this situation seriously enough." His gaze at each of us was somber. "I want to leave you with this message." He hesitated for effect. "I sincerely believe, without reservation, that this visit is perhaps one of the most momentous events, not only of our Bureau careers, but of our entire lives."

We left then, quietly, leaving him alone with the American flag, President Eisenhower, the enduring frown of the Director, and the responsibility for providing tough ice cubes and brown lap robes folded just so and elevators that were always waiting for the Director and Mr. Tolson when they were ready to board them.

At the time of Mr. Hoover's visit to Texas in 1959 he was sixty-four years old. He had been Director of the Federal Bureau of Investigation since 1924. His closest friend and colleague, Clyde Anderson Tolson, was five years younger. Mr. Tolson had joined the FBI in 1928 and, to my knowledge, had never worked in the Field, only at SOG as Mr. Hoover's closest subordinate. In my recollection, he is a gray figure, always in the background. Not many people outside the Bureau, or inside for that matter, knew much more about Mr. Tolson than the facts set forth in his biography in *Who's Who in America*. I can add only a few details gleaned from my brief contacts with him during his Texas visit in 1959.

He seemed to function mainly as a confidential secretary, whispering in the Director's ear and writing in a small notebook. He addressed Mr. Hoover in conversation as "Eddie" and seldom took his eyes off him when they were together in public, as though he were continually awaiting a signal. For ten years prior to joining the FBI in 1928 he had been a private secretary to three different Secretaries of War. He drank Grant's Scotch (the eight-year-old) and his hobby was inventing mechanical gadgets. He mentioned in conversation that he held a patent on a snap-on bottle top that would prevent the fizz from escaping from a bottle of club soda after it was uncapped and also a patent for mechanical windows that would close automatically when it began to rain. In physical appearance he was approximately the same height as Mr. Hoover, about five feet nine inches tall (which *is* under six feet), but he was more slender. Ralph de Toledano has said Mr. Tolson was "Hoover's security blanket and flunky more than an operating assistant." De Toledano never worked for the Bureau. He might have revised that opinion if he had. A man who could send you to Bloody Harlan, Kentucky, for two years for an idle remark in conversation had plenty of clout as an operating assistant.

Most people are aware that Mr. Hoover lived and died a bachelor. I have never heard or read that Mr. Tolson ever married. During their long association in the FBI allegations were occasionally made, either directly or by innuendo, by people outside the Bureau, that an "unnatural" relationship existed between them. These allegations infuriated Mr. Hoover. He attributed them to "public rats," "guttersnipes," and "degenerate pseudo-intellectuals." When received by agents in the Field, such allegations had to be handled very carefully.

On Thursday, November 5, Tom Carter went to Dallas and brought back the borrowed Cadillac. He was to keep the car at home until time for the trip. "Driving that thing worries me," he said. "I'm afraid I'll have a wreck and have to pay for it." He went to an insurance agent and bought a short-term policy covering every catastrophe he could think of that might happen to the Cadillac, the driver, and any occupants during the time he would have the car in his possession.

On Friday, November 6, late in the afternoon, the SAC telephoned Fort Worth and asked for Carter. Since Carter was out of contact somewhere in the Cadillac, the SAC gave me his message. His voice sounded fainter than usual. "They're here," he said. "They just called from the airport."

I almost jumped from my chair. "The Director and Mr. Tolson?"

"No, no, no!" The SAC's voice rose with exasperation. "The inspection team!"

"Who's the chief inspector?"

"A fellow named Fly," said the SAC.

"Anybody know him?" I was hoping that Inspector Fly might have a close friend in the Dallas office who could soften him up, or perhaps a bitter enemy who might know something very bad on Inspector Fly, something that could be used against him as a club in case he tried to get too tough.

"Yes," the SAC's voice faded again. "I know him. He's a brand-new inspector and he's a protégé of the assistant director I told you about. You know, the one who doesn't like me." Then the SAC hung up.

When Carter returned to the resident agency office from driving practice I told him that the inspectors had arrived. His smile froze. The combined onslaught of Director, Mr. Tolson, and an inspector bearing a contract shook his composure. "Let's see," he said, "I've got about a year's sick leave accrued. I could probably get a doctor to certify I was off my rocker or on the verge of a nervous breakdown or something and go to a nut house for a year if they tried to transfer me. Or, if they sent me to Oklahoma City or San Antonio or some place close by, I could always get a cheap room at the YMCA and come home on weekends until I got my time in. That way I wouldn't have to move my family and sell my house." He looked at me thoughtfully. "How much time do you have left?" he asked, as if he did not know.

"Eleven years," I said. "Eleven years, eight months, and twenty-seven days."

"Well, look at the bright side," he said. "You're still fairly young. You could probably adjust to snow and sleet and an icy wind blowing off the Great Lakes. You might have Eskimo blood and not realize it."

Then it was Sunday, November 8, 1959, and I was sitting behind the wheel of a Bureau Ford parked on the edge of the landing area near one of the American Airlines entry gates to the terminal building at Love Field, Dallas. Nearby the 1960 Cadillac four-door sedan gleamed like a black jewel in the sun. Half a dozen agents had spent hours that morning dusting and polishing it. Inside were the two black umbrellas and two envelopes of road maps and brochures, which the SAC had checked personally to make sure that exactly the same items were in each. The weather bureau had forecast clear, warm weather for the next three days, so the SAC, after a telephone consultation with Nick Callahan, had decided to eliminate the lap robe. However, he had placed a dustcloth in the glove compartment for Carter's use during stops.

The Washington plane bearing the Director and Mr.

Tolson was making its landing approach, according to information from the terminal control tower relayed by an American Airlines public relations man. Standing near the Cadillac were the SAC, Carter, and three agents who were to whisk the visitors' luggage from the plane to the trunk of the Cadillac. All were thin. All wore dark suits, white shirts, subdued ties, and hats. Except for the hats, they looked like a group of pallbearers waiting for a hearse.

Within a few minutes the big airliner, its four propellers flashing, touched down on the runway and taxied toward us. The SAC led his contingent of bagmen forward, leaving Carter standing alone near the Cadillac. When the plane stopped near the terminal entry, the SAC stood at the foot of the stairway which had been rolled out and secured to the plane's door. The three agent baggage-handlers ran around to the other side of the plane, accompanied by an airline employee in coveralls who would open the compartment door so that they could get the right luggage off first. Callahan had telephoned the SAC shortly after the Director and Mr. Tolson departed from Washington that morning to describe their luggage. The Director had two cases of bright aluminum—a two-suiter and a smaller bag. Mr. Tolson had a single large brown leather suitcase of the three-suiter size.

The Director and Mr. Tolson, both wearing dark snap-brim hats and overcoats, were among the first passengers down the steps from the plane. After shaking hands the SAC led them toward the Cadillac. I recognized the Director's famous bulldog profile. He walked briskly, swinging his arms from the shoulders to and fro in front of him. Mr. Tolson followed slightly to the Director's rear, and I noticed his singular way of walking. He had a gliding, measured tread with accompanying body and arm movements, which reminded me of a skin diver walking on the floor of a tank full of clear water. They stopped briefly to shake hands with Carter. Each carried a small leather envelope-type briefcase, which neither relinquished. As expected, the Director entered the car first and sat on the right side of the rear seat. The SAC closed the door for him and escorted Mr. Tolson around the back of the car to the left rear door so that he could take the "death seat" behind the driver.

The three agent baggage-handlers hurried up and stored the luggage in the trunk. When the trunk lid had been closed, the SAC personally tested it to make sure the latch had caught securely. Then he moved to the left front of the car and waved at the occupants. This was a farewell to the Director and Mr. Tolson and a signal for Carter to get moving.

The Cadillac bearing its precious cargo slowly skirted the edge of the landing area while I followed at a discreet distance in the Bureau Ford. It turned right at the main entrance to Love Field and headed west on Mockingbird Lane. Sunday traffic was fairly heavy, so I stayed only two cars behind. Approaching the turn to Highway 77, the Cadillac's left tail light began blinking its signal, and it moved carefully into the protected left-turn lane to stop and wait for a green arrow. When the arrow flashed on, the Cadillac made the dreaded left turn safely and headed up the ramp to the Stemmons Expressway and the straight shot to Austin, 194 miles away. The Director, accompanied by his good right arm, Mr. Tolson, was now in the heart of the Field, courageously facing all the hazards of dirty ashtrays, soggy mattresses, wrongly folded lap robes, and perilous left turns that such a venture entailed.

13

America's Number One G-Man Meets the Stringless Yo-yo

It would be interesting to relate that during the drive to Austin something catastrophic happened to the Cadillac—a wreck, a flat tire, or a mechanical failure —and that I, in the words of my SAC, swooped down, scooped up the Director and Mr. Tolson, and gave my cover story, which was "I just happened by, et cetera, et cetera, and recognized you, and am available to take you to your destination." Nothing of that sort happened. The Cadillac stopped only once during the four-hour trip. That was for the Director and Mr. Tolson to use the rest room in the Gulf Service Station on the traffic circle at Waco, a city approximately halfway between Dallas and Austin. The rest room had been inspected just a few minutes before their arrival by one of the resident agents at Waco. He and the station manager had made sure it was spotless.

While the two distinguished visitors were answering nature's call, Carter had a service station attendant wipe off the windshield and all the windows while he person-

ally worked on the interior with his dustcloth and
cleaned Mr. Tolson's ashtray.

The resident agent from Waco and I observed these
proceedings through binoculars from the parking lot of
a drive-in restaurant half a block away. When the two
came out of the rest room, they stood by the car con-
ferring briefly.

"I guess Lewis and Clark are discussing the route,"
said the Waco resident agent sourly. Apparently his task
of touching up the rest room prior to their arrival had
not appealed to him.

Then the two jumped into the Cadillac and the trip
continued.

Darkness was beginning to fall as we approached
Austin. I notified the Austin resident agency by radio of
our impending arrival and followed the Cadillac as it
angled off the freeway at the Sixth Street exit, turned
right on Sixth to Congress Avenue, *right* on Congress
one block to Fifth Street and *right* again to park parallel
to the curb at the main entrance of the Stephen F. Austin
Hotel, which stands on the northeast corner of Congress
and Fifth.

I saw the tall figure of Cal Hanson, one of the Austin
resident agents, standing outside the lobby entrance to
greet the visitors as they emerged from the car as soon
as it had stopped. Then Carter and another agent, who
I learned later was Rod Ruffin from the San Antonio
office, got the bags from the trunk and followed as
Hanson led the way through the lobby to a waiting
elevator. There was no dilly-dallying at the desk for the
Director and Mr. Tolson to fill out registration cards.
Hanson had already done that for them.

I left the Ford parked at the curb behind the Cadillac
and waited in the lobby. A few minutes later Carter,
Hanson, and Ruffin returned on the elevator. Carter was

smiling and relaxed as usual, and Ruffin appeared calm, but Hanson looked apprehensive.

"I hope we get through tonight and tomorrow without getting gored," Hanson said. "This has been a major project. I had to change some of the furniture in the suite to comply with Callahan's instructions. I had to rent a double bed and two mattresses from a furniture store. I hope that the mattresses aren't too hard or too soft and that the pillows are O.K. LBJ wanted to put them up in the Presidential Suite at the Driskill Hotel across the street gratis, but Callahan said no, the Director had to stay in the same hotel where he was making his speech. So we had to rent this suite for three nights and change the furniture. I don't know who's going to pay for all this extra stuff."

We wandered into the hotel restaurant for coffee.

"Anything happen on the way down?" Hanson asked.

"No," said Carter. "They ate some sort of hard candy from their briefcases and talked, and every once in a while Tolson would lean forward and look over my shoulder at the speedometer to make sure I wasn't exceeding the speed limit."

"Did they talk to you any?"

"Some," said Carter. "They wanted to know how big Austin was and about the University and about the football team. I gave it all a big buildup."

Hanson winced. "Play it down, play it down," he said. "They might get the idea I've got it too good here."

Hanson was in his office of preference with about two years to go until retirement. He was afraid that the Director or Mr. Tolson might suspect him of "complacency" if his situation appeared too attractive and ship him out. I could understand his viewpoint. I was glad that the Director and Mr. Tolson were staying at the Stephen F. Austin Hotel in Austin that night and not the Hotel Texas in Fort Worth. They might have found the room service abominable and blamed the resident agents, or their suite might have had one of those tricky Miami toilets that flushed upward to disaster.

"They seemed to like the flowers and the basket of fruit in the room, didn't they?" Hanson asked. "And the whisky was O.K., too, wasn't it? Jack Daniels black label and Grant's eight-year-old? That's right, isn't it?"

"Relax, Cal," said Carter. "Everything's all right."

"I hope so," said Hanson, "but you never know. I think I better stay here at the hotel tonight instead of going home. They might decide about midnight they want to go sightseeing and hold it against me if I wasn't here."

Carter, Ruffin, and I had dinner that night in an Italian restaurant on Sixth Street a few blocks from the hotel. Hanson declined to join us, saying he was on a bland diet and would go home to dinner. He promised to return later and spend the night at the hotel. We were glad he was staying around. If the Director and Mr. Tolson did decide in the middle of the night they wanted to go sightseeing, his services as guide would be indispensable. After dinner we returned to the hotel to turn in early. We looked forward to the next day with anticipation and foreboding.

The next day, Monday, had an air of comedy about it that lingers in memory to this day. Carter, Hanson, Ruffin, and I met in the hotel coffee shop at 8 A.M. to eat breakfast, talk about what was going to happen, and try to plan for emergencies. We understood that Senator Johnson would appear at the hotel about 10 A.M., pick up the Director, and take him for a brief tour of the city. The tour included making a speech by the Director before the assembled student body at Huston-Tillotson College, a predominately black institution, which would allegedly endear Senator Johnson to the Negro electorate. We did not believe Mr. Hoover had been informed of this impending speech, but we certainly did not intend to mention it to him.

During this coffee shop conversation we decided that two Austin agents in a radio-equipped Bureau car would follow the cars carrying the Director and the Senator and report their whereabouts to my Bureau car parked at the curb in front of the hotel. The Director and the Senator were supposed to return to the hotel in time for the luncheon at 12:15 P.M., and the Director would make his United Fund speech. After the luncheon we presumed—and Cal Hanson sincerely hoped—the Director and Mr. Tolson would return to Dallas in the Cadillac.

Shortly after 10 A.M. Senator Johnson arrived at the Fifth Street entrance of the Stephen F. Austin Hotel in a pale green 1959 Chrysler Imperial. He charged into the lobby leading a pack of half a dozen young men who seemed to be his retainers. The Senator was tall, well over six feet, with wide hips and waving arms. He was wearing a gray suit and greenish sport shirt buttoned at the collar without a necktie. He was hatless and wore cowboy boots. He seemed to know every hanger-on in the lobby and greeted them all, bounding about, head bobbing and arms shooting out in all directions, shaking hands with two people at a time and embracing others. When he was not squeezing hands and hugging shoulders, he was displaying a small card to everyone. This card attested that a recent electrocardiogram he had taken had been normal. Senator Johnson had suffered a severe heart attack several years before; he now wanted to exhibit medical evidence of complete recovery and the physical capability to serve his country in the highest office in the land.

After completing a circuit of the lobby the Senator and his party crowded into an elevator and disappeared upward. They soon spilled out again into the lobby accompanied by the Director and Mr. Tolson. Senator Johnson personally escorted the Director. Much the taller of the two, he had his arm wrapped around the Director's neck as though putting a headlock on him and dragged him through the lobby to the sidewalk outside, where a crowd had begun to gather to see what all the excitement was about. Senator Johnson pulled the Director this way and that, introducing him to everybody in sight, without for a second releasing his hold on his guest's neck.

A crippled boy in a wheelchair pushed by two other boys stopped on the sidewalk across the street, and Johnson yelled at them, "Come over heah, boys! I want you all to meet J. Edgar Hoover, America's Number One G-Man!"

When the boys hesitated, several of the Senator's retainers ran across the street, took possession of the crippled boy and his wheelchair, and hurried him across the street.

As the Director shook hands with the crippled boy, the crowd cheered and clapped.

"Attaboy!" yelled Senator Johnson, trying to shake hands with people and still hang on to the Director. "He's America's Number One G-Man!"

Mr. Tolson, who had been gliding about in the background, now motioned to Carter for a whispered conversation. As Carter walked back toward the Cadillac, Ruffin and I moved in on him.

"The Director will ride with the Senator in the Imperial," said Carter. "Mr. Tolson and some of the Senator's aides will follow in the Cadillac. We're going to Huston-Tillotson College, where the Director will make a brief speech. The Director doesn't want to make the speech, but the Senator is insistent, so he's going to do it. Then we come back here for the luncheon. Mr. Tolson is beginning to be concerned about time."

Suddenly, as though a starter's gun had been fired, everyone dashed to cars. Johnson dragged the Director into the back seat of the Imperial and several of his aides hurried Mr. Tolson into the Cadillac. Away they went, straight east on Fifth Street, the Imperial in the lead followed by the Cadillac. An Austin FBI car raced behind to radio the movements of the Senator and his captive Director.

Rod Ruffin, Cal Hanson, and I were left at the hotel with an important mission. We had to ensure that an elevator was waiting with the door open to receive the Director when he returned to the hotel. The words of Nick Callahan had been explicit. "The elevator must be ready and waiting when he walks into a hotel lobby anywhere. He will not tolerate waiting for an elevator."

The Stephen F. Austin was not a new hotel; it had only three elevators in the lobby bank. Ruffin and I implored the operators to be alert for the return of the group, then we took turns contacting the agent in my car who was listening to radio reports on the where-abouts of the Imperial and the Cadillac.

Judging from the radio messages, the Senator was leading his guests on a helter-skelter tour of Austin reminiscent of his lunging, arm-waving, hand-shaking tour of the hotel lobby. They dashed first to Huston-Tillotson College, where Senator Johnson led the Director onto the stage of an auditorium filled with several hundred black students. The Director made an impromptu ten-minute speech while Mr. Tolson and the rest waited. Then the Senator and the Director returned to the Imperial and whizzed north, closely pursued by the Cadillac and Bureau radio car, to the Villa Capri, a new and luxurious motor hotel on the interstate highway just east of the University of Texas campus. The Senator did not reveal that he had still another speech planned for the Director. On arrival at the Villa Capri he lured the Director from the Imperial on the pretext of introducing him to a small group of state officials lunching there and again led him onto the stage of another large auditorium —this one filled with mostly white faces—for another impromptu ten-minute speech.

Back at the Stephen F. Austin Hotel we were having problems of our own. Just as we received word from the radio car at the Villa Capri that the Senator's group was almost ready to return downtown, an old man in white cap and paint-stained overalls, carrying two stepladders and a plank, appeared in the hotel lobby from some hidden back entrance. He set up the ladders in front of the elevator bank and placed the plank across the ladder tops, forming a large scaffold which blocked two of the elevators completely; then he prepared to begin painting.

Rod Ruffin hurried over to stop him but the painter was apparently deaf. He just kept nodding and smiling and going on about his business. At Ruffin's frantic summons, the hotel manager came running. The manager and Ruffin dragged the surprised painter down a hall leading off the lobby, while I followed with ladders, plank, and paint cans, and we found him an inconspicuous place to begin his work.

Suddenly, the lobby door burst open and the agent from the radio car ran in bawling, "They're here! They're here!"

Ruffin and I ran back to the elevator bank. Our adventure with the painter had diverted us for a critical moment from our primary mission. The doors of the only elevator car at lobby level were just closing. Ruffin leaped recklessly between them and with superhuman strength pushed the doors apart.

The lobby doors flew open again. Senator Johnson, still hugging the Director around the neck, led the herd across the lobby to the elevator where Ruffin stood like Hercules holding the doors apart. From nowhere came a small, middle-aged woman, apparently a hotel guest, headed for the elevator. Ruffin and I tried to block her out but failed. Although small, she was powerfully built and was probably a veteran of many a year-end department store sale. She fought past us to be swallowed up and flattened against the rear wall of the elevator car by the crushing press of men.

Remaining in the lobby, I watched the elevator doors close and then watched the numbers flash on and off as the car moved upward, finally stopping on the top floor, where the luncheon was to be held.

A few minutes later Ruffin returned, harassed and rumpled. "We had one hell of a time keeping her from stopping the car at her floor," he reported. "She kept yelling, 'out, please, out, please,' but we went right on past to the top. I bet she could kill us all. Mr. Tolson may have noticed what was going on but I don't think that Mr. Hoover and Senator Johnson did. LBJ kept hugging the Director's neck and telling what they were going to do after the luncheon, and the Director kept saying, 'No Lyndon, no, Lyndon, no, Lyndon,' but Lyndon never stopped talking for a single second. We finally all got off at the top floor, leaving the lady on the elevator mad as hell."

What Senator Johnson wanted the Director to do after the luncheon was make a flying trip to Johnson's ranch near Stonewall, about fifty miles from Austin, and then fly back to Dallas in Johnson's private airplane—a twin-engine Beechcraft—for the overnight stay. The prospect of dashing down to the ranch and then back to

Dallas in a small, bumpy airplane apparently did not appeal to the Director.

Ruffin and I, trying to recuperate from our elevator labors, wandered out to the curb on Fifth Street and found another problem. When the group had returned from the Villa Capri, the curb at the hotel entrance was temporarily occupied by a departing airport limousine. The Cadillac and Imperial had double-parked in the street to disembark their passengers. When the limousine departed, Carter parked the Cadillac at the curb, leaving a space behind for the Imperial. But the driver of the Imperial, whoever he was, had gone on into the hotel leaving the Senator's car parked in the middle of Fifth Street.

A uniformed city policeman assigned to directing traffic at the hotel entrance went to the Imperial to move it. Discovering that the keys had been taken from the ignition, he hurried into the lobby to get them from the driver, only to find that the driver, along with the rest of the Johnson party, had disappeared upward on the elevator. Now the officer was red-faced and angry, calling Senator Johnson and his aides all kinds of uncomplimentary names.

"Maybe we can push it out of the street," I said.

"I'll be goddamned if I'll push the goddam car. I'm not being paid to push a goddamned senator's car," said the officer. "I'm going to call a wrecker and have it towed away."

"I wouldn't do that," said Carter. "The Senator might go to the Chief of Police and cause you a lot of trouble. It's not worth getting into trouble over."

"I'll get some of the agents and we'll push it so it's sort of double-parked alongside the Director's Cadillac," I said.

"No, by God!" said the officer. "We'll leave that

Imperial sitting where it is and if some half-assed sergeant or city official comes by here and makes a beef, I'm going to say that's Senator Lyndon Johnson's car and if you don't like where it's parked, then by God you go upstairs and take the matter up with the Senator." The officer kept frowning and mumbling to himself. Obviously his love of order was deeply offended by Senator Johnson's apparent disregard for it. "That damned stringless yo-yo," he said. "I'll never vote for him again."

About an hour later Senator Johnson's group erupted into the lobby once more. The luncheon was over. The Senator still had the Director by the neck in a death grip and dragged him through the doors to the street, where he began introducing him again to everyone in sight.

I learned later that in his luncheon speech Mr. Hoover had warned his listeners that the time had come to stop "coddling" young hoodlums—juveniles who committed serious crimes. He also warned that the Communist Party remained "an integral part of a treacherous international conspiracy against God and freedom directed from Moscow." He lauded Senator Johnson as "an outstanding public servant and one of the most able lawmakers in the nation's history."

Texas Governor Price Daniel had made him an "honorary Texan" and Austin Mayor Tom Miller proclaimed the day J. Edgar Hoover Day.

Mr. Tolson floated over to Hanson and Carter. "Eddie has decided we are to fly to the ranch in the Senator's plane," he said. Mr. Tolson's expression and tone of voice did not project relish for the prospect.

"Carter," he said, "you will take the Cadillac and our luggage back to Dallas. Before you leave here, telephone the agent in charge at Dallas that he must arrange to pick us up on our arrival at a place at Love Field called . . ." he scanned his notebook, "Southwest Airmotive. It's a place on the field where privately owned aircraft land. I don't know our exact hour of arrival, but presume it will be between 5:30 and 6 P.M. It is my information that it takes about forty-five minutes to fly from the ranch to Dallas in the Senator's plane, and the pilot will notify the airport tower by radio of our time of arrival when we depart from the ranch. If you cannot drive the Cadillac back to Dallas and reach Love Field within the allotted time—strictly observing the speed limits—then the agent in charge at Dallas must make other arrangements for a car to pick us up there immediately upon our arrival and transport us to the hotel. Is that clear?"

"Yes, sir," said Carter.

"Now, in regard to our hotel expense," said Mr. Tolson. He took a folded fifty-dollar bill from his pocket and handed it to Hanson. "I don't know the cost of the accommodations, but this should be sufficient. Please send me a copy of the receipt and any change in a personal note. I suggest you take the flowers and fruit from the suite to your family. The fruit basket has not been touched, nor the whisky. If expense was involved in regard to the whisky, I suggest it be returned to the store for credit." He shook hands with Hanson and then floated away to post himself near the Director and the Senator, who were standing in the street by the Imperial shaking hands with people who converged on them from all directions.

Hanson stood with the fifty-dollar bill in his hand. The suite had cost thirty-five dollars a night but it had been necessary to rent it for two extra nights because of the football game. Also, the cost of replacing some of the hotel furniture with rental pieces had to be paid. Well, as the SAC at Dallas had said, "Problems arising in the San Antonio division have to be solved by the San Antonio division."

A few minutes later the group crowded into the Imperial. Senator Johnson pushed the Director into the "death seat" and jammed himself in next to keep his left arm wrapped around the Director's neck. The Imperial took off with a screech of tires. At the next corner, Brazos Avenue, the driver zoomed through a red light in a lightning left turn and disappeared northward.

The policeman kicked the curb in frustration. "One of these days!" he said. "One of these days I'm going to give him a ticket for reckless driving, I don't give a goddam who he is!"

Ater loading the luggage into the trunk of the Cadillac, Carter and I started the long drive back home. We left Hanson the task of telephoning Mr. Tolson's instructions to the SAC at Dallas.

On the outskirts of Dallas about 5:30 P.M. I called on my radio to the base station in the FBI office and was informed that the SAC and Jack Bain were at Southwest Airmotive awaiting the imminent arrival of Senator Johnson's plane. They planned to transport the Director and Mr. Tolson to the hotel in Bain's personal car. Our instructions were to proceed to the Sheraton and deliver the luggage to the suite. I honked Carter to a stop on the side of the road and delivered the message. We drove into Dallas to the Sheraton and delivered the luggage. The doorman then showed us where we could park the Cadillac at the curb of the curving driveway just past the main entrance. I noticed there was another black Cadillac limousine parked nearby. I presumed this was a parking area reserved for VIPs, not for the common run of guests.

Shortly after 6 P.M. Jack Bain drove up to the main entrance in his personal car, a white 1959 Ford four-door sedan, and the SAC and the visitors got out and entered the hotel. Agents stationed inside jerked the lobby doors open as they approached. Another agent had an elevator waiting with the door open. This time no Senator Johnson hung on the Director's neck and no muscular little lady appeared to fight her way into the same elevator. The Director and Mr. Tolson ascended in majesty, accompanied only by their own retainers.

Soon the SAC came down on the elevator and joined us in the lobby. He was smiling. "Everything seems to be going fine," he said. "Senator Johnson must have shown them a hell of a time at his ranch. Flew them over the place in the airplane and then landed and took them riding in a jeep. Everything seems fine in the suite here. The Director especially liked the telephones in the bathrooms. I guess he likes to sit on the can and yak long distance. All we have to do now is get them on the plane tomorrow and we're home free."

We went into the coffee shop to discuss plans for next morning.

"How is the inspection going, Boss?" asked Carter.

The SAC shook his head gloomily. "It's really too early to tell but this fellow Fly has a contract for me as sure as we're sitting here. The first thing he told me was that he intended to review *every* pending case in the office."

That did sound ominous. Generally speaking, inspectors reviewed only a fraction of the pending cases, stopping when they felt they had found a sufficient number of errors on each supervisory desk to create the illusion for SOG that they had really given the office a going over. If they reviewed every pending case, rules and regulations being as multitudinous as they were, they could find hundreds of errors. Undoubtedly there was a contract out for the SAC.

At 7 A.M. next morning the SAC, Carter, Bain, several other agents, and I met in the Sheraton coffee shop. The

Washington flight was not due to leave until 10 A.M., but the SAC was an early riser and liked to have everyone on the job ahead of time. He was the last to arrive and seemed upset. "Tom," he said, "I thought I made it plain you were to keep that Cadillac immaculately clean at all times. I checked it this morning and the interior was filthy. I cleaned it out."

Carter stopped eating breakfast long enough to say, "The Cadillac is clean. I'm going out in a little while to wipe the dew off of it."

"It was filthy, filthy," the SAC said again. "There were some rags in there and tin cans and God only knows what else. I threw that junk into a trash can. I thought I was going to have to whip the doorman. He thought I was a car prowler or something." The SAC hurried away toward the telephone booths to notify the office where he was, in case Inspector Fly wanted him for anything.

Carter resumed eating his breakfast. "I wonder how the SAC got into the Cadillac. I left it locked up. I have the keys in my pocket."

Then we both stopped eating and looked at each other silently. The answer had struck us both at the same time. The SAC had cleaned out someone else's Cadillac.

After breakfast we went out and looked over the cars parked on the curving drive. Sure enough, there were two black 1960 Cadillac four-door sedans parked there. Ours was farthest away, half-hidden by a large shrub.

"Anything going on?" Carter asked the doorman.

"Not much," the man said, "Earlier this morning some nut got into Maria Callas's Cadillac over there and started throwing stuff out of it. I had to chase him off. She may get mad as hell about it. He threw some of her personal stuff from the car into the trash can before I could stop him. You know these opera celebrities. They've got a bunch of nuts following them around. Not like Mr. Hoover. I bet there's just a few people who even know he's in town. Just the ones who *need* to know. That's the way for a real celebrity to travel."

"Right," said Carter. "We're going out now and wipe the fog off the windows of our car and warm up the engine."

The doorman nodded his approval. "You guys think of everything. I've seen professional chauffeurs park cars here overnight and not find out they had a dead battery until they had their big shots aboard and tried to start the engine."

"My God!" said Carter to me, "Imagine the horror of loading up those two and finding out you had a dead battery."

Carter unlocked the Cadillac. To our relief the engine started immediately with a healthy roar. We let the motor idle while Carter wiped off the windows with paper towels from the hotel rest room. I wiped out the interior with the dust cloth from the glove compartment and made sure the ashtrays were clean.

Back in the Sheraton lobby at 8:45 A.M. the SAC had forgotten the Cadillac cleaning incident because a new problem had arisen. "The damned airplane is going to be late," he said. "Today, of all days, the damned airplane has to be late." He seemed unable to stop pacing back and forth cracking his knuckles. "But one thing may save us. Billy Byars and his wife from Tyler are coming in to see the Old Man off, so maybe they can keep him entertained. Bain has arranged it so they can visit in the VIP room until the flight leaves."

B. G. "Billy" Byars was an oil millionaire from Tyler, Texas, 96 miles east of Dallas. He and his wife were old friends of the Director from La Jolla or somewhere.

At 9:30 A.M. we loaded the Director and Mr. Tolson

into the Cadillac again, bag and baggage, and drove to Love Field. This time the SAC accompanied them, riding in the front seat beside Carter. I rode with several more agents in a car behind. We had to make certain that the Director's and Mr. Tolson's luggage went into the plane baggage compartment last so that the agents in Washington could get it off first. Carter managed the trip to Love Field without a left turn by making three extra right turns around the Sheraton to get the Cadillac pointed in the proper direction. Those of us in the following car could see that the Director was riding in the right rear seat, Mr. Tolson was in the "death seat," and the SAC rode in front with his head turned toward the passengers, talking constantly.

In the American Airlines VIP room at Love Field an attractive middle-aged lady wearing a mink coat threw her arms around the Director and said, "Welcome to Texas, J. Edgar!" Then she hugged Mr. Tolson. She was accompanied by a prosperous-looking man in a dark suit. These people were Mr. and Mrs. Billy Byars from Tyler.

The Director was delighted to see them. The news that the flight was late, allowing him additional time for a visit, delighted him still more. He sat in a large chair by a window and dominated the conversation with a rapid-fire description of his visit to "Lyndon's" ranch. "I really didn't want to go," he said, "but Lyndon wouldn't take no for an answer. Lyndon is the only man in the world who can talk me down on anything. I would hate to have a million dollars and have Lyndon try to sell me some real estate in Iceland."

Mr. Tolson, seated on a hassock almost at the Director's feet, watched for signals. Mr. and Mrs. Byars sat on a couch with the SAC. We baggage-handlers and retainers, along with an American Airlines public relations man, stood in the background listening to the words of the living legend.

The wonders of Lyndon's ranch were numerous, according to the Director. He and Clyde had seen deer, wild horses, and what looked like a wildcat, all running loose on the prairie and in the forests of Lyndon's domain. Lyndon had driven them around in a jeep, bouncing across fields and fording streams. "A fantastic experience!" said the Director. "Perhaps a little frightening at times. Of course, I was not frightened. I'm a Presbyterian and believe in predestination, but I think Clyde was frightened."

Mr. Tolson could not confirm or deny his fright; the Director's voice rattled on and on like a runaway machine gun, drowning out everyone else.

The Director said that when they had flown from Austin and first tried to land on the strip at the ranch, they had been unable to do so because there were several "wild horses" on the strip. He made a swooping gesture with his hand when relating how they zoomed low over the strip and mimicked Lyndon shouting orders on a bullhorn at people below to chase away the horses so they could land. "It was fantastic! Fantastic! The most fantastic day I've ever spent in my life!"

He was still telling how fantastic it had all been when the Washington flight was called. Regretfully he said goodby to Mr. and Mrs. Byars. Then, accompanied by the SAC, he walked to the aircraft boarding steps, with Mr. Tolson gliding along just behind. Carter and I stood near the Cadillac and watched the agent baggage-handlers scamper around to the other side to make sure their bags went into the compartment last. At the foot of the steps the Director and Mr. Tolson shook hands with the SAC and then boarded the plane with the Director leading the way.

The SAC walked briskly back to Carter and me. "We're not out of the woods until the bird has flown," he said.

We watched the big plane taxi slowly out the runway to the flight line and then lumber away, faster and faster, until, finally airborne, it dwindled to a dot in the distant sky and disappeared.

"O.K.," said the SAC, getting into the Cadillac with Carter. "That fire's out. Drop me off at the office so I can see how bad Inspector Fly is cutting up the place. Then take this jalopy back where it came from."

Carter and I returned the Cadillac to the dealer and went back to Fort Worth. "I'm glad that's over," said Carter. "I'd rather work a million dollar bank robbery with no suspects than do that again."

The Dallas office inspection, under the supervision of Inspector Fly, went on and on for a long time, and his team ferreted out a large number of "substantive errors." As I have said, substantive errors, like mortal sins, could mean eternal damnation in the Bureau, especially for SACs. Most agents who did an appreciable amount of work usually made several substantive errors in the course of a year's work. They buried them in investigative files the way rats bury their nests in grain bins. The assiduous sifter could find most of them, given the time and the inclination.

Inspector Fly may not have found all the subs in the Dallas files, but he found an imposing number, including one allegedly committed by me. (Please note the use of the word "allegedly." Like the Director I have never owned up to making any sort of error in the FBI, and I do not intend to begin now.) Fly enumerated all these subs in his inspection report to his superiors at SOG. The report concluded with the recommendation that the SAC be demoted and transferred and that a number of agents, including myself, be severely censured.

The SAC said, "I've told the wife to get ready to sell the house again and have another garage sale. The rest of you guys better disperse and dig in. When that report hits the Old Man's desk, there'll be nothing left of this office but a blackened, smoking crater."

In the meantime, we decided to have an office party. The Director and Mr. Tolson must have carried miniature bottles of bourbon and scotch in their luggage, because we found the empties in the suite wastebaskets. They had not opened the Jack Daniels or Grant's we left for them. Sid Bowser raffled off the two bottles at the office party for twenty-five cents a chance and made about $25 a bottle. That took up the slack on some of the expenses we had incurred as a result of the visit.

After the party, we waited. But the days turned into two weeks and the rocket never crashed in. Nothing happened. Finally the SAC cautiously contacted his anonymous friend at SOG, the one who had first warned him of the contract. The friend said he would tap the grapevine. His signal came next day. When the inspection report with its hostile recommendations crossed Mr. Tolson's desk he took up his pen and wrote, "The Director recently visited the Dallas office and found no such conditions as described herein. No administrative action required." He sent the report back to the Inspection Division without further comment.

The assistant director who had issued the contract saw at once how wrong he had been. Having misplaced confidence in a subordinate, he swatted Inspector Fly to the bricks for incompetence and put him on probation. Then he wrote a glowing letter to the Director praising the administrative capabilities of the SAC at Dallas.

As a result of the combination of Director's visit and

office inspection I received a letter of commendation and a letter of censure in the same mail delivery. The letter of commendation was a blanket one sent to the SAC and all the agents who had participated in making the Director's visit to Texas such a "memorable experience."

The writer of the letter of censure at SOG must have read the "good" letter prior to preparing his bad one. It is quite possible that the same supervisor wrote both letters. I had never before received such mild remonstrance. The letter, over the Director's signature, alleged that I had failed to "afford continuous investigative attention" to a White Slave Traffic Act case assigned to me and politely suggested "in the future you should exercise a somewhat higher degree of promptness in reporting the results of official investigations so as not to be charged with a similar delinquency again."

I showed the letters to Carter and he laughed. "You have to keep your sense of humor," he said. "Just keep on thinking of this outfit as a sort of nutty vaudeville show and you'll make it without getting an ulcer."

Then I showed the letters to the SAC and he said, "The good letters cover up the bad letters just like debit and credit, see? The more good ones you get, the more credit you got. The goons fly in, catch you mixed up in a little sub, start to write you up and then, lo and behold, they see a recent good letter in file. 'Go easy,' they say to themselves, 'the Director thinks this old boy's O.K. Better not disagree with the Director. Might be fatal.' It's all part of the halo effect."

The SAC suddenly somersaulted out of his chair and did a handstand. Then he walked around the room on his hands, his change and other pocket junk falling on the floor around him, his necktie hanging down in front of his face while his legs kicked wildly in the air.

14

"Have a Good Time in Florida, Gentlemen"

The two of us were sitting in a corner of the drab reading room of the FBI Academy at Quantico, and Howard was telling me the troubles he'd had as SAC of the Director's front office for the past eight months. Howard had recently been removed on short notice and transferred to Mobile as SAC.

"When he gave me the news, he called me in without warning and said, 'I want you to understand this is *not* a promotion!' Of course, it's a relief to be out of there but I've never had any experience in running a field office. I may screw up and become a big target for the inspectors to shoot at after I get to Mobile."

"Why did he kick you out of his office?"

"Oh, it's almost too silly to talk about. I know what it was, but he never mentioned it."

"Didn't you ask him about it?"

"Oh, no, no. You don't ask him about anything like that. The Hebrews never questioned Jehovah when he told them to get the hell out of Egypt, did they?"

"They were going to the Promised Land," I said.

"That's where I'm going," said Howard. "Mobile *is* the Promised Land. I'm going to be his personal representative in Mobile. It can't help but be better than that office on the fifth floor of the Justice Building."

Howard had been an agent for fifteen years, and for fourteen of those years he had been assigned as a supervisor at SOG: a clod if there ever was one. Now he was going out to run a field office. He did not know anything about running a field office and he would have much preferred to find another niche or cranny at SOG to hide in, but that stint in the Director's office had made him a marked man, and he was on his way to the Field whether he liked it or not.

"An idiot can run a field office," said Howard. "That's what the Old Man told me when I left. 'An idiot can run a field office, if he's an obedient idiot. Just run it exactly as I tell you and you can't go wrong,' he said. But I keep thinking maybe that's not quite so. It might be a disloyal thought, but maybe things go on in the Field the Director doesn't know about."

"You'll make it all right, Howard," I said. "You're beginning to think straight already."

"Well, my wife isn't happy about leaving the Washington area, of course. Everything has gone so well for me in the Bureau up to now. I guess I flew a little too close to the sun and the wax melted like that guy and his kid who made the wings."

"Did you volunteer for the job in the Director's office?"

"Oh, hell no. Anybody would know better than to do that. I've worked in the Administrative Division ever since I came to SOG fourteen years ago. I liked my boss there just fine. I worked on the budget and personnel requirements and things like that. I had my own little office and a secretary and everything was pretty good."

"What happened?"

"Well, it was just one of those things that creep up on your blind side, you know. When I came up for a regular in-grade raise, the supervisor in the Administrative Division who reviewed my file said, 'I see you haven't been in to see the Director in almost five years.' " Howard paused reflectively and said, "I wonder if that son of a bitch set me up."

"Why would he do that?"

"Hell, for all kinds of reasons. You guys out in the Field are naïve as hell. You don't know what goes on up here. You see, he knew that the assistant director in charge of the division and I were personal friends who played bridge together. Maybe he was jealous. Also, I recall that several years ago, during a self-inspection of our division, I found some of his procedures weren't exactly kosher as far as the Manual was concerned. When I pointed them out to him, he got sort of defensive and upset like I was trying to shaft him. But I thought that was all water under the bridge. Come to think about it, that might be the reason he made that observation about going in to see the Director."

"What did you do after he said it?"

"Well, I went back to my office and thought the matter over. Maybe this guy was right, I thought. Maybe the Director would think that I was avoiding him. Like that young Navy officer in *Mister Roberts* who was on the ship for months before the captain even saw him. There's some sort of rule of thumb—I don't know where it started—that you should go in and pay your respects every two years. Maybe it started with his practice of pulling in SACs every year or so for an ass-chewing and the guys assigned abroad when they came home on leave.

And, actually, I was about to come up for a promotion. The assistant director and I weren't giving it any publicity, but he was going to recommend me for a grade raise. I thought maybe I ought to go in and let the Old Man see I was still alive, just so he wouldn't be surprised when my name came across his desk, in the near future I hoped."

"Didn't you realize how risky it was going in there?"

"Yes, yes, but I was confused. It was one of those things that seemed like a good idea at the time, that turned sour. Like throwing a forward pass. Can a quarterback ever call one back like he had a rubber band on it? Don't tell me now how risky it was. Where were you the day I was worrying trying to make up my mind what to do?"

"Don't get pissed off at me about it."

"Pissed off? What do you know about getting pissed off? You've sat down there in that cream puff resident agency for years, taking two hours for lunch when you felt like it, playing golf two or three times a week when you're supposed to be working. I've been out on inspections. I know how resident agents are—lying, malingering bastards."

"Howard, Howard, relax," I said. "Tell me about going in to see the Director."

"All right, all right, I went in there. Like a damn fool. He was very cordial. Seemed to know all about me and all that. Oh, I knew some clerk had synopsized my file and he had read it over just before I came in. But it was very flattering just the same. Oh, he was in a talkative mood. Mostly about Bobby Kennedy."

"What did he say?"

"Mostly about his being an adolescent horse's ass. How when he and Mr. Tolson went to pay their courtesy call on the new Attorney General they found him sitting behind his desk with his coat off throwing darts at a target across the room."

"A dart thrower? Say, is it true like they say that the Administrative Division has this blindfolded ape that throws darts with agents' names on them at the map to make transfers?"

"Listen, Joe, that's the kind of talk the Director simply will not tolerate. I'll give you the word for your own good. You've been telling that crazy story around here to the New Agents. I've heard you. And that Bottom Five thing, too. If those stories got to Art Buchwald or one of those pinko liberal humorists, the Director would bounce your ass. He might fire you by teletype, veteran or not. He almost lost his mind when Buchwald wrote that column that he didn't exist at all, that he was a mythical person made up by the *Readers Digest*. If a story like the ape throwing darts or that Bottom Five thing got to Buchwald . . ."

"Tell me about Bobby and the dart board."

"Well, the Director said that when he and Mr. Tolson went in, Bobby was sitting in his shirt sleeves behind the desk throwing darts and kept on doing it all the time they talked. In other words, he did not give the Director his undivided attention. The Director said he had served under a score of Attorneys General during his time in government and it was the most damnably undignified conduct he ever witnessed. He was especially disturbed because Bobby frequently missed the target and the dart stuck in the wall paneling. 'He was like a child playing in a Dresden china shop,' the Director said. 'It was pure desecration. Desecration of government property. The problem was that the child could not be disciplined. He happened to be the Attorney General of the United States and his brother was President.' The Director said that he and Mr. Tolson cut their visit as short as possible and both agreed that it was the most deplorably undignified conduct they had ever witnessed on the part of a Cabinet member. Of course, I had already heard about the AG telephone incident, but he didn't talk about that."

"What was that?"

"Oh, for years the Attorney General has had a direct telephone to the Director's office. It was always kept on Miss Gandy's desk. When Bobby called and got Miss Gandy he told the Old Man to put the phone on his own desk. He said when he called on that phone he wanted to talk to the Director, not the Director's secretary. Of course, for years Mr. Hoover never had to take any crap off an Attorney General. He just dealt directly with the White House and let the AG go fly a kite. But this was something new. This AG was the President's brother. It would be very difficult to wire around the President's brother. So the Old Man, very reluctantly, had the phone moved to his desk. Something funny came up about that phone later, after the assassination . . ."

I bored in like Mike Wallace interrogating Colson or Ehrlichman. "You say you had been assigned there at SOG for fourteen years, that you knew how risky it was to go in and talk with the Director and you went in anyway?"

"Yes, yes."

"Well, what in hell happened? What did you do or say to him that got you transferred in there as SAC of the front office or whatever they call it?"

"I don't know. I thought and thought about it later trying to figure out what it was and I never could. He talked a lot about loyalty and about what a terrible thing disloyalty was. When he talked about disloyalty he mentioned the assistant director who had been Bobby's friend. The one who tried to back up Bobby in his story that Bobby didn't know about a lot of the wiretaps. 'Judas Iscariot,' the Director called him, 'Judas Iscariot.' "

"Judas Iscariot? Does the Director think he's Jesus, for Christ's sake?"

"Hold it down, Joe! Hold it down. You'll get us both fired. You've been out in the sticks too long. That nutty SAC here at Quantico may have this place bugged."

"We could always go up in the shower room like they do in the movies and turn on the water. The roar would probably drown out . . ."

"Stop clowning, for God's sake. This organization has been a good career for me up till now. I had my own little office and my own secretary and I understood the budget and the personnel requirements and now I have to go to the Field to an óffice that's probably full of clowns like you. I don't know anything about the Field!"

"We'll teach you, Howard," I said. "It will take about a month to six weeks to break your will and get you to seeing things our way. Just keep on scanning your memory bank and try to retrieve what it was that you said . . ."

"I don't know. I don't know. I've thought and thought. Maybe it was the loyalty bit. Just before I left the office that day, he looked me square in the eye and asked, 'Are you loyal to me?' "

"What did you say?"

"What in the hell do you think I said? I said, 'Yes, yes,' babbling like an idiot. I would have fallen down on my knees and kissed his big toe if he had told me to."

"What happened then? Did he just say, 'Go out and take over the front office, you're it,' or did he . . ."

"No, no, the transfer came unexpectedly. Two days later, when I came back from lunch, there was a note saying the assistant director wanted me in his office right away. I thought to myself, 'Oh, boy, he's got my grade raise!' But when I went in, it was a different story. He looked at me sort of unfriendly and asked me how long I had been unhappy working for him. Unhappy working for him! Hell, this guy has been my rabbi. When I was just a lowly supervisor he took a shine to me and got me transferred into his office. He got me promoted to grade fifteen, and sometimes he let me sit at his desk and answer the phone when he was on annual leave or off sick. 'What have I done wrong?' I asked him. 'What have I done wrong?'

"He handed me a memo which said I was being transferred immediately as SAC in the Director's front office. I felt hot and cold flashes. I started to shake. I must have turned pale, because he got up and brought me a glass of water. 'My God,' I said. 'My God, what have I done?'

" 'You've just got yourself transferred to the hottest seat in the Bureau, that's what,' he said. How right he was. How right he was."

"When did you have to go to the Director's office?"

"Immediately," Howard said. "The memo said, 'immediately.'

" 'Run, do not walk, to Mr. Tolson's office,' the assistant director told me. 'Don't even stop by your own office for anything. If you hesitate even slightly Mr. Tolson might say that you don't act like you're 200 per cent eager for the promotion. Then the Director would ship you out to the Field on the bricks. I've done all I could for you, but you screwed it up and now you're on your own. In that new job you'll have to prove your abject loyalty and utter devotion every minute of every day. Don't forget that. One false move and you're finished.' I asked about the promotion in his office I was supposed to get. The one I really wanted. He just laughed. 'You're on your way to Oz, now,' he said. 'Just follow the yellow brick road. Follow the yellow brick road.'

"On my way out, I passed the guy who had suggested I go see the Director. He had already heard the transfer news. He looked at me sort of respectfully. I'm sure he never thought when he made his suggestion that I would be promoted into the Old Man's front office as SAC. He probably hoped, when he made the suggestion, that I would go in there and screw up and be transferred out of the Administrative Division and he would get my job. It worked out that way, anyhow. He later got the promotion I was supposed to get and now he plays bridge with the assistant director. But that's life in the jolly old B. I went on down and reported to Mr. Tolson and thus began my eight months of hell in the Director's front office."

"What was so bad about it?"

Howard took off his glasses and rubbed his eyes wearily. "God, everything. You just can't do anything right in there. And it seemed like that every time I got going on something that was halfway important, I had to check out one of those damn ambulance sirens."

"Ambulance sirens?"

"Yeah. You know the tours that are always going through the Bureau? Well, in hot weather when all those high school kids come to Washington, they gang up outside the Ninth Street entrance to be shuttled through in groups. They've all been drinking soda pop and eating hot dogs and stuff and a lot of them aren't used to the Washington heat and they get sick and throw up and some of them pass out on the sidewalk or in the halls of the building. When this happens to a kid, the nurse handles it, generally, but when one of the adults falls out, the nurse almost always calls an ambulance. So whenever I heard an ambulance coming up Pennsylvania

Avenue I had to call the nurse or the Tour Room to find out if somebody had fallen out, and if so, who, and immediately inform the Director before the ambulance stopped below his office there on Ninth Street. If an ambulance stopped and no one had already told the Director why, it was my ass."

"Why does he want to know stuff like that?"

"He wants to know everything, that's why. *Everything*. And I couldn't leave the office unless he did. His schedule had to be my schedule. But he never told me ahead of time what his schedule was going to be, see? I was afraid even to take sick leave to go to the dentist, unless he was out of town. And it's a seven-day-a-week job, buddy. I had to go down to the office on Saturdays to look through his mail and put all the important stuff in a briefcase and take it personally to his house. And I did the same on Sunday for teletypes. And Tolson would call me at home at all hours. If I had to go to the drug store at night, I had to leave word with the Bureau switchboard operator. My wife and I got so we never went anywhere. We just stayed home and waited for a telephone call."

"What kind of stuff did you handle in there?"

"Anything the Director told me to. A lot of the time the stuff didn't come from him directly, however. It came from Tolson or Miss Gandy. A lot of it sounds funny just talking about it, but it was serious in there, I kid you not."

"Like what?"

"Well, like one time he visited this ceramic manufacturer millionaire somewhere—the guy manufactures bathtubs and commodes and lavatories—and the Director took a liking to one of the super-fancy toilets in the guy's guest house. He passed the word to the guy that he sure did like that commode, so the guy sent him one for his home. Naturally the Director wanted it installed in his bathroom immediately. I had to get a plumbing contractor right out there, while the Old Man was at the office, to take out the old one and install the new one."

"Big deal. One of the guys I work with in the RA can do that sort of work himself. Does it all the time. He can install hot water heaters, mount commodes, all that stuff."

"Yeah, but it was too high."

"Too high? What was too high? You mean the price?"

"No, no, nothing wrong with the price. It was free. The goddam commode was too high off the floor. Tolson said the Director was very unhappy about it. He told Tolson he felt like he was sitting on top of Mount Everest with his legs hanging down on each side. Tolson said that the commode in the manufacturer's guest house had been exactly the right height for the Director. He told me to call the SAC there at once and have him go personally out to the guest house with a tape measure and measure the height of that commode. The SAC was to call back this information immediately. Then I was to have the commode reinstalled at the right height—immediately. Luckily, Tolson said, it was Friday, and he and the Director were leaving town for the weekend. 'That's a lucky break for you,' he said to me. I knew then who would be blamed if it wasn't right the second time. So I called the SAC and got him moving and alerted the plumbing contractor that we were going to have to make some quick changes. Then I went out to the Director's house and measured the height of the commode in his bathroom. It was some throne. When the SAC called in the commode height from the guest house, sure enough it was about two inches lower than the one in the Director's house.

"When I told the plumbing contractor we were going

to have to lower the commode two inches, he said that meant he would have to tear up a lot of the bathroom floor and reset a lot of tile and he was going to have to have a lot of help to do that over the weekend.

"I said no sweat and called the assistant director in charge of the lab and told him the problem and that we needed help. He pissed and moaned but finally sent half a dozen guys out to help the plumber. They were mad, having their weekend ruined like that. They tore up the floor, reinstalled the commode, and reset the tile. I guess they set it at exactly the right height because Tolson said the Director used it on Monday and had been very complimentary."

"They sent Bureau employees out to work on his house?"

"They did it all the time," said Howard. "The lab services all his appliances, and once when a light bulb went out, he raised so much hell that they decided to replace every bulb in the house about every two weeks. They even built him a patio one weekend."

"A patio? How did that happen?"

"Tolson just said the Director *wanted* it, that's all. The Old Man visited someone who had one that he liked. The lab sent technicians out to measure and photograph it and next weekend, while he was gone somewhere, they had a dozen or more guys out at the Director's house digging and hammering like a bunch of beavers. One of the Director's neighbors was so impressed he asked the Old Man who the contractor was. The neighbor said he had never seen laborers work like that before, from sun-up to sundown, Saturday and Sunday, hardly taking time out to eat. Stuff like that isn't hard to handle when you know exactly what the Director wants. It's when he wants something and you don't know exactly what it is that it's hard. Like his office TV set. One evening he said to me as he was leaving the office, 'There's something wrong with my TV set. Get it fixed.' I called the lab and they came up and got the set, tested it out, and couldn't find anything wrong with it. But to be on the safe side, they replaced a lot of the tubes and stuff, reinstalled it in his office and tested it. It worked fine. But next day he told me again when he was leaving that the TV set had not been fixed. I called the lab again and the guy checked it out and said it *was* working O.K. I told him he could tell that to the Director. He got upset and pulled all the guts out of the set and replaced everything. But next day, sure enough, the Director told me it wasn't working right and this time he really acted mad."

"Why didn't you ask him what was wrong with it?"

"Ask him? Don't be silly. Nobody asks him to explain anything. You just say, 'Yes sir,' and then try to figure out what he wants. Well, I was desperate. I described the problem to Miss Gandy. She went into his office and came back in a few minutes. 'The trouble is,' she said, 'when he turns on the set it takes almost a minute before the picture comes on. He wants the picture to come on as soon as he snaps the switch. Immediately, you know. He doesn't want to wait.'

" 'The set has to warm up,' I said. 'The set has to have time to warm up.'

" 'That's your problem,' she said. 'I'm just telling you what he said was wrong with it.'

"So I called up the guy in the lab again and laid it out for him. 'Jesus Christ!' he said, 'Commercial transistorized television is at least two years away. What's he expect, a miracle?'

" 'Yes,' I said.

"So the lab guy called somebody at RCA and that night they took the set up to the lab and installed some sort of dummy switch that kept the picture tube hot all the time. The lab guy said it would mean the tube was really on all the time and would burn out twice as fast, but the picture would come on bang just as you flipped the switch. I guess that solved the problem because there were no more beefs about the TV, but it meant the lab had to make another tickler card to remind them to change the TV tube periodically, the way they did the light bulbs in his home and office."

"Wasn't there any fun in there at all?"

"Well," Howard almost giggled, "I figured out a good way to settle some old scores, to give some guys the shaft who had tried to shaft me in the past. I figured out a way to do it with the routing block stamp on the Director's incoming mail. The routing block is a stamp that lists the names of all assistant directors. Every piece of mail that goes in to him is supposed to have the routing block stamped on it so he can check off the names of the assistant directors who are supposed to get copies. Whenever a piece of mail comes to his desk without that stamp, it makes him fighting mad. He'll chop people into hamburger after that happens. So whenever some guy was scheduled for an appointment, some guy who had tried to give me the business in the past, I would send in a piece of mail with the routing block missing—half an hour or so before the guy was supposed to appear. When he went in, the Director was steaming like a tea kettle. He would chew the guy's ass good and sometimes put him on probation."

"That's a chickenshit thing to do, Howard."

"Let's face it. This is a chickenshit outfit. I made one little false move and got the shaft. Why not give it to somebody else? Chickenshit is the name of the game up here, my boy. Whimsical, musical chickenshit."

"What took you out, Howard?"

"Well, it's so goddam stupid I hate to even talk about it."

"Oh, come on, Howard."

"Well, just between us, then, but don't let it go any farther. It happened just when I thought everything was going O.K. I thought I had proven my abilities with the commode and TV deals and even Mr. Tolson smiled at me occasionally when we met in the hall. I began to think that if I could just walk the tightrope a year or so longer I might really make my mark in the Bureau. You know, be promoted to assistant director, maybe. But I must have a latent death wish or something. One day I opened my mouth and the craziest thing popped out. It happened a couple of weeks ago when they were getting ready to leave on their annual trip to Miami. They go there every January, you know. After seeing that their bags had been safely stowed in the car taking them to the airport, I helped them on with their topcoats. The Director was in a great mood, talking away about some restaurant he likes in Miami Beach where they have such good sea food and lime pie. Since the Director was in such a good mood, Mr. Tolson was in a good mood too. I was in a pretty good mood myself. The prospect of having both of them gone for two or three weeks must have unhinged me, because that's when I said what I did."

"What did you say, Howard?"

"I said 'Have a good time on your trip to Florida, gentlemen.' They sort of stopped talking for a second but then started again and went on out. I got the impression that there was a little coolness in the air but didn't think it was important. I was so relieved at having them both gone I was almost out of my mind. Then, about an hour later, my old boss, the assistant director in charge of the Administrative Division, called me on the phone. 'Howard, you've managed to escape. How did you do it?'

" 'What do you mean?' I asked.

"The assistant director said, 'I thought you were the fairhaired boy since that commode deal, but you are being transferred to Mobile as SAC. Mr. Tolson called me from the airport. He said this was not a promotion. He wanted that clearly understood. Not a promotion. Evidently you made them mad about something, just mad enough but not too mad. What did you do?'

" 'All I said was have a good time on your trip to Florida.'

" 'Oh, hell,' the assistant director said. 'That's what did it. You inferred they were going down there to have a good time or enjoy themselves. They never own up to anything like that. They aren't going to Miami on vacation, they are going there to inspect the Miami office.'

" 'Bullshit,' I said. 'That's bullshit and you know it. They stay in a beach house in Miami Beach and don't go anywhere near the Miami office.'

" 'Howard,' the assistant director said, 'your thinking is just too fuzzy to make it in the Director's office. Maybe you belong in the Field. I'm sending you In Service to delay your departure long enough to get your family ready for this transfer. And compose some sort of ass-kissing letter to the Old Man, Howard, thanking him for the opportunity to work in such close proximity, et cetera, et cetera, such an inspirational experience, et cetera, et cetera, and thank him for the transfer. You know, really bury your nose in his ass. Then when the goons fly into Mobile in six months or a year, maybe they won't be carrying a contract for you. You do what I say, Howard.'

"Well, I'm trying to be philosophical about it," Howard said. "If I can sweat it out in the Field as a SAC for the next five years I'll have it made. But even if they bust me to the bricks, I have to stay in. I've got so much time invested, you know. Before I left to come down here I went back and talked to the assistant director and asked if he thought it might do any good for me to go in and talk to the Old Man and tell him I was sorry I hadn't measured up and so forth, and ask for another chance. 'No, Howard,' he said. 'You just go down there to Mobile and try to survive. That's about the best you'll ever be able to do in the Bureau now. Survive, that is.' "

We sat there silently for a while, each thinking our own thoughts about survival and so on. Then it came to me that I had digressed away from something Howard had alluded to earlier in the conversation. "I worked some on the Kennedy assassination investigation, Howard. What was it you said about something funny happening to the phone to the Attorney General's office after the assassination?"

"That was kind of funny," Howard said. "It really showed how much the Old Man hated Bobby. You know I said Bobby had made him take the AG phone off Miss Gandy's desk and put it on his, so that when Bobby called he would have to come running. Well, on that Saturday after the assassination, after Jack Ruby shot Oswald in Dallas and President Johnson had issued an executive order for the FBI to investigate, the Old Man and several of the assistant directors were in his office making plans. The Old Man had talked with President Johnson personally several times that day. In the middle of the conference, the AG telephone on his desk rang. Mr. Hoover didn't answer it, so everyone tried to ignore the ringing. When it finally stopped, Mr. Hoover said,

'Put that damn thing back on Miss Gandy's desk where it belongs.' They called the telephone company and had it done right away. I don't think that he ever spoke to Bobby after that. He damn sure never talked to him over that phone."

15

Getting In to See The Man

It generally annoyed a SAC when one of his agents went in for a private chat with the Director while visiting Washington. Those sneaky ones who did not reveal their plans ahead of time were especially upsetting. When an unexpected memo came down from SOG informing the SAC that one of his boys had slipped in to see The Man, the SAC would frantically try to find out what they had talked about.

The really sneaky ones, on being questioned, would answer vaguely, "Oh, he just asked me how the office was being run and stuff like that," and then refuse to say what his answers had been.

Some agents went in to see the Director every time they were in Washington as part of a continuing strategy to keep their SACs at bay. One of these characters once said to me, "It's just self-preservation. The SAC will lay off you because he's afraid you'll run in and tell the Director some wild story about him."

Once, after being forced by an abominable SAC to cover a lot of inane leads on one of the Bureau's "Ten

Most Wanted Fugitives," known in the trade as the "Top Ten," I conceived the idea of a "Bottom Five" program, the Bureau's "Five Least Wanted Fugitives." I thought that establishing such a program might give recognition to those agents who never seemed to get to work big cases and make them feel good. I broached the idea to the SAC and said I was contemplating telling the Director about it, the next time I was at SOG.

"I wish you would!" he snarled. "You ever see those Vietnamese monks on television who doused themselves with gasoline and then struck a match? They burned themselves to charcoal dummies. That's what you'd look like when you came out of his office—a charcoal dummy —if you ever laid on him that Bottom Five program or the alligators in the sewers or the ape with darts."

Well, I let him bluff me out of it. Who wants to end up looking like a charcoal dummy?

Going in to see the Director was dangerous; the unexpected was always happening in his office, but that did not stop many with personal problems to present.

Most agents had to wait a long time for transfer to their offices of preference. The most dangerous and courageous way to circumvent this long seniority wait was to go in and hit up the Old Man directly. Although fraught with danger, it sometimes paid off. It paid off for Red Mullins, another Boston Irishman who had chosen the Bureau instead of the priesthood and found himself, twelve years later, assigned to Chicago where he did not want to be. Mullins and his wife had a dream: Fort Lauderdale, Florida. Fort Lauderdale was not a field office. It was a mere speck of a resident agency on the big toe of the United States, in the territory covered by Miami. Mullins knew that it was too much to expect that the blindfolded chimpanzee, left on his own, would hit such a tiny mark with his dart.

Mullins had something vaguely resembling a rabbi at SOG, a low-echelon supervisor who had shared his joys and woes in New Agents. So when Mullins went In Service he confided his plan to hit up the Director to his rabbi.

"Very dangerous," said the rabbi, jerking and quivering and looking around apprehensively. "He may ship your ass to Timbuktu just for asking."

"I got nothing to lose," said Mullins. "No place could be worse than Chicago." Then Mullins described his Fort Lauderdale dream, evoking images of powder-white beaches, endless horizons of blue ocean, bikini-clad bronzed bodies lolling in the eternal sun.

The rabbi sighed and looked out the window at gray January in Washington. "If it works, I might hit him up myself."

"What's a good subject to talk about to get him in a good mood before popping the question?"

The rabbi thought for a long time. "Food," he said at last. "Food and restaurants. The Director has strong opinions about both. Last year when I went in, he had just come back from New York where he had eaten at the Waldorf. He said the Waldorf served the finest food in New York, especially desserts. He was especially fond of their pastries, I recall."

"Yeah," said Mullins. "I don't see how I could go wrong talking about food."

The rabbi gave him a bleak smile. "With the Director, you can go wrong talking about Santa Claus or the Virgin Mary, if you say something he doesn't agree with."

Mullins planned his strategy. He would tell the Director that on a recent wedding anniversary, he and his wife had gone to dinner at the Waldorf because they believed it served the finest food in New York, especially desserts.

"My wife and I are very fond of the pastries there," he rehearsed himself. That should open the door to pleasant vistas. Then, after he had visions of sugar plums dancing in the Director's head, he would hit him up for the transfer to Fort Lauderdale.

At last the day came. Mullins was summoned from class. Fortune smiled. Noisette said The Man was in a good mood. Sunlight streamed in through the windows of the inner office, and when Mullins entered, Mr. Hoover leaped to his feet like a jack-in-the-box to shake hands.

Early in the conversation, the subject of food and good places to eat came up. The Director said, "Until my last trip there, I always thought that the Waldorf had the finest food in New York. But the last time I ate there, the food was abominable!"

"Isn't that a coincidence?" said Mullins. "My wife and I had dinner there on our last wedding anniversary and she said it was the worst meal she ever ate. Especially the pastry. She said they served her the soggiest piece of pastry she ever saw in her life."

The Director smiled. "Your wife is a woman of great perception." Then he gave Mullins a ten-minute, rapid-fire rundown on his favorite dishes and restaurants.

"Do you know of any good restaurants in Fort Lauderdale?" Mullins asked.

Indeed, the Director did. He named several.

Then Mullins made his pitch, and afterward the Director scribbled in his file. Mullins and his wife were two of the bronzed bodies lolling on the beach at Fort Lauderdale before the month was out.

Of course, all those who yearned for promotion *had* to go in. There were never any written tests or standards or formalities for promotion. The beginning point was the Director. The aspirant went in and expressed his burning ambition. In a matter of minutes the Director would decide whether or not the supplicant was worthy. If favorably impressed, the Director would scribble something like "appears to be supervisory material" in his file, and he was on his way. But if the size of his head or the color of his socks or the shape of his ears offended the Director, the supplicant could forget his ambitions as far as the Bureau was concerned. He was damned to the Field for the rest of his days.

The SACs and ASACs all had to go in when they visited SOG. Some of their sessions were stormy. One SAC was so unnerved by the Director's broadside that, instead of finding the exit on being dismissed, he walked blindly into the Director's closet.

When someone went in just to pay his respects, that could also backfire, as in the case of Howard, who was promoted to SAC of the Director's office and then exiled to Mobile. There was also the case of Ron Mell.

"It was really a bum decision on my part," Mell said. "I had just been made a field supervisor and given a pay raise in the office where I had been assigned for several years. My teen-aged kids liked their school and had their friends. My wife liked our house and neighbors. It was the first house we'd ever had that was big enough for all of us—five kids, you know. Then I got this crazy idea I ought to go in and see the Director when I went In Service, just to pay my respects. I put in my name for a visit. Of course, one of those SOG guys asked me a lot of questions about what I wanted to see the Old Man about, if I had any problems my SAC couldn't solve and all that. I finally convinced him that I just wanted to say hello, like I had said. So one day they called me out of class to go to his office. I was amazed that he was so cordial. You know how you hear so many horror stories about his being a holy terror. My God, he's a whirlwind talker. Something got him started on the Marine Corps, about how much he admired Marine discipline. He said that was the trouble with young people today, lack of discipline. The student riots seemed to be bugging the hell out of him. He said all those students should be sent to a place like the Marine base at Parris Island to learn discipline. Discipline was very much on his mind that day, and Parris Island. Just before I left, I made a stupid observation. I said, 'As a former Marine who went through Parris Island, I can assure you it's quite a place.' I must have been crazy to say that! I hated Parris Island! I almost throw up when I think about it. I still have nightmares about the drill instructor I had there. He was psycho as hell, trying to kill us all to prove *he* had balls. A couple of days after I got back to the field office, the SAC received a letter notifying him I was being *promoted* to supervisor at SOG. Promoted? My wife's been screaming at me ever since I told her. She hates Washington. She lived in a house trailer there with four kids while I was in New Agents. She says she's not going. The kids say they're not going. They all stand around and yell at me when I'm home. I'm afraid to refuse this crazy promotion. He'd probably get mad and transfer me to Butte. I told my wife I would go on up there and live at the YMCA while she sells the house. She says she's not going to sell the house and doesn't care where I live. 'Why don't you go back to Parris Island?' she asked me last night. 'Maybe you and the Director could learn discipline together.' "

Well, that was the way it was when he ruled at SOG. As the cringing pilgrim approached the heights of Olympus, a bush would burst into flame and a voice would speak: "No grade thirteen! I will never send you to Boston! Not supervisory material! Come to SOG! Go spread the gospel in Fort Lauderdale!"

Now he is dead, buried in state by the President he wanted in 1960 but did not get. Mr. Tolson, Director for a day, retired. LBJ is buried at the ranch, commemorated by a huge, pyramid-like library on the University of Texas campus, not far from the Villa Capri.

Carter and I and the SAC who invented the halo effect and many of the others—the connivers, the baggage-handlers, the observers of small incidents—are retired. We are doing our acts on other stages.

Time has solved many of our problems. The Director and Mr. Tolson no longer have to worry about soggy mattresses or waiting for elevators or those dangerous left turns. LBJ doesn't have to worry about capturing the black vote or winning the Presidential nomination. He ultimately did both—then everything went blooey in Vietnam.

Best of all, from a selfish point of view, we proles and bagmen no longer have to worry about office inspections, substantive errors, letters of censure, or, as the SAC used to say, "the prospect of being busted and transferred to an igloo resident agency just south of the Arctic Circle, et cetera, et cetera."

Epitaph

At 8:30 A.M., Tuesday, May 2, 1972, Mr. Hoover's housekeeper, Annie Fields, found him lying on the floor beside his bed. She summoned his personal physician, Dr. Robert V. Choisser, who confirmed her fears that he was dead. The official medical report gave the cause of death as "hypertensive cardiovascular disease"—in layman's language, a heart attack.

The "bums, rats, craven beasts, vermin from the jails, vultures, slobs, kooks, misfits, pinkos, rabble-rousers, Commies, bleeding-heart judges, sob-sister parole boards, sentimental yammerheads, pseudo-intellectuals, so-called liberals, enemies of law and order, scavengers, and garbage collectors" were suddenly silent. He had fought them hard for forty-eight years as Director of the FBI, but time had finally run out on him.

As a former lieutenant colonel in the U.S. Army Reserve, it was his right to have requested in his will burial in Arlington National Cemetery, where so many notables of his generation already lay. Because of his eminent position, the request undoubtedly would have been granted. He had not chosen Arlington. He designated Congressional Cemetery in Southeast Washington, where his parents were buried.

On Wednesday, May 3, his body lay in state in the Capitol Rotunda, the coffin resting on a catafalque built for Abraham Lincoln. At the memorial service in the Rotunda Warren E. Burger, Chief Justice of the United States, read a eulogy.

Next day the nation saw on television his funeral at the National Presbyterian Church. As I watched, I could hear his voice saying, "Of course I was not frightened. I'm a Presbyterian and believe in predestination."

When I saw his coffin surrounded by uniformed members of the armed forces as pallbearers, I yelled at the set, "This is ridiculous!" Where were the clods and trolls from SOG, in their Bureau uniforms—conservative business suits, white shirts, and subdued neckties? Where were the assistant directors, the inspectors, the SACs? Why were these soldiers and sailors carrying him his last mile? They never fought in the great war between SOG and the Field. All they knew was Vietnam.

They presented the flag which had draped his coffin to Mr. Tolson, who also inherited most of the Director's worldly goods. All he left in the way of an immediate family were two Cairn terriers and the FBI.